M000283051

ENOUGH?

How Much Money Do You Need For The Rest Of Your Life?

Paul D. Armson

First published in Great Britain in 2016
by Envision Your Money Limited

© Copyright Paul Armson

All rights reserved. No part of this publication may be reproduced, stored
in or introduced into a retrieval system, or transmitted, in any form, or by
any means (electronic, mechanical, photocopying, recording or otherwise)
without the prior written permission of the publisher.

The right of Paul Armson to be identified as the author of this work has
been asserted by him in accordance with the Copyright, Designs and
Patents Act 1988.

The book is sold subject to the condition that it shall not, by way of trade
or otherwise, be lent, resold, hired out, or otherwise circulated without the
publisher's prior consent in any form of binding or cover other than that in
which it is published and without a similar condition including this
condition being imposed by the subsequent purchaser

Dedication

To Lynn
My soulmate
My best friend

Contents

Introduction	9
Enough?	15
A Smart Career Move?	19
The Early Days	23
It Happened On A Thursday	27
The Penny Drops. Thanks Mum.	31
What Are You Waiting For?	41
Understanding Your Bucket	47
What's Going To Happen To YOUR Bucket?	69
Which Money Type Are You?	75
The 'Not Enough's'	77
Mr & Mrs Not Enough	79
The 'Got Too Much'	83
Mr & Mrs 'Got Too Much'	86
The Just Right's	91
Mr & Mrs Ten Years Younger	94
Mr & Mrs Are We There Yet?	97
Mr & Mrs Do It Yourself	99
What's The One Thing Everybody Wants?	103
What If You Are There Already?	113
Relax. It's Easier Than You Think!	117
What's In? What's Out?	121
What's Coming In To Your Bucket?	127
What's Going Out Of Your Bucket?	131
Not Enough? Are You Paying Yourself First?	137
A Special Word to Small Business Owners…	143
A Word About Investing	151
Risk and Investments	155
The Man Who Liked Financial Porn	159
The Truth About Financial Advice	163
Finding The Right Adviser	171
This Case Study Is Quite Upsetting	174
What's Most Important To You?	179
Going To The Gym!	185
About the Author	189

Introduction

How much money do you really need for the rest of your life?

This book will help you to find out.

The fact is the majority of people have no idea where they are heading financially. They may have assets, investments, and/or high levels of income, but most people have no idea what it all means, or what sort of financial future awaits them.

On the one hand they don't want to retire too early, only to discover their money runs out. On the other hand they don't want to retire too late and end up working when they could have been playing! Then again, because of savage taxes due on death, they don't want to die with too much money ... but they're afraid to spend it or give it away!

What we all need to know is: "How much money do I need for the rest of my life?"

This book helps you discover 'how much is enough' - for YOU.

Having an insight into how much money we actually need, can be enlightening. It can put you in control. Knowing how much is ENOUGH will give you the freedom to live your life smarter. After all, life is not a rehearsal; it needs to be lived to the max.

In the following pages I'll introduce you to the concept of Lifestyle Financial Planning: a way to help you find this freedom. Using simple step by step instructions this book will guide you through the process of developing your own financial plan.

I'll also introduce you to the concept of the Number.

You know lots of numbers. Your phone number, your PIN number, your account number, your National Insurance number. But do you know the most important number of all?

It's the amount of money you need for the rest of your life - not just to survive but to live it to the full.

It's different for each of us, of course. So what's your *personal* number?

Is it a million? Two million? A lot more? A lot less? Is it five million? Ten million? How much do you really need?

You need to know.

Here's the thing. You can probably have a lot more fun at 55 than you can at 85. So the earlier you can understand your Number the better. But how much do you need, to do everything you want to do, without ever having to worry about cutting back?

Without knowing your Number, how can you plan? How can you decide what's best?

This book (and supporting resources) will help you find your Number. And when you've found it it will help you see how to build it, nurture it, protect it - and most importantly - ENJOY IT!

In fact, I'm hoping this book will change your life.

You'll find it is a quick read - for a reason. I want it to be the first book about money that you feel inspired to read from cover to cover.

It was never intended to be a literary masterpiece. It isn't crammed full of confusing industry jargon and there is no expectation for its reader to know an ISA from a hedge fund. There are no chapters educating you on the myriad of financial products and investments; no tedious ramblings about the pros and cons of active versus passive investing; no boring chapters on the impact of a falling FTSE and a rising oil price on your pension plans … it is not that kind of book.

Instead, this book is about YOU. It's about what YOU want.

I firmly believe that good financial planning is the essential tool that can help you to get and KEEP the life you want; to envision your future and find real peace of mind in this hectic world.

I'm hoping that the feeling you get when reading this book will be rather like having me sat next to you, talking you through my ideas. So it is intentionally delivered in a conversational style, which will hopefully help to make a potentially overwhelming subject really accessible to everyone. I've included some real life case studies to help illustrate the key messages, and I hope you'll find my 'bucket' analogy priceless. It is my intention that you will find inspiration, motivation and 'direction' inside these pages.

Why have I written this book?

After years of being a successful Financial Planner, and more recently training other Advisers to deliver more meaningful outcomes for their clients, I feel it's time to step up to the mark. This is due to my increasing frustration with the self-serving vested interests of the Financial Services Industry.

I believe it's time consumers understood the 'Truth About Money'. I want to help more people understand what they need to know most - the things the Financial Services Industry doesn't necessarily want you to know. I want to dispel the myths that the world of financial planning is daunting and convoluted. I want to empower everybody to take control of their own future without having to worry about dealing with unscrupulous or expensive advisers and unpredictable, overly risky investments.

This book is intended to simply and clearly explain what good Lifestyle Financial Planning really is, and why it is so important to understand your Number: how much is ENOUGH. By doing so, it will help you to secure your financial future with more clarity and more peace of mind than ever before.

By the end of this book you may even know a lot more about financial planning than some financial advisers!

I hope it inspires you to think about - and do - what's possible.

Paul

Chapter One

Enough?

Imagine. You have more than enough money to last you for the rest of your life.

Imagine that.

You need never worry about money again. Ever.

Financially, everything is perfect. You can keep living the life you want - and you're NEVER going to run out of money.

The only trouble is...

...you just don't know it!

If you didn't know you were going to be OK, how would you live your life?

Chances are, you'd still worry about money. You'd go without. You'd skimp on the nice things in life.

Perhaps, if you were still working, you'd plan to retire at 65 when in fact, you could retire at 55. Perhaps you'd keep working when you could be playing. Perhaps you'd be stressed out and tired, doing a job you no longer enjoy, when instead, you could be having fun.

Already retired? Perhaps you'd often worry about your money and about how long it was going to last.

Perhaps you would not treat yourself and your family when you could easily afford to do so.

Or worse, you might spend money - and then feel guilty for doing so!

Imagine that! Paying for a wonderful holiday, treating your loved ones - and all the time thinking to yourself: *"I shouldn't really be doing this!!"*

That's no way to live or to have fun. Thinking and worrying about your money is the best way to miss the most important thing of all - the precious moment!

Miss enough precious moments and you miss a lifetime!

Here's another thing: you'd probably take more risk with your investments than you really need to. After all, you'd always be seeking 'a good return' on your money.

Sunday mornings might see you stressing over the money pages. You'd easily fall prey to the financial propaganda -

'financial porn' I call it. Financial scaremongering fills newspapers and websites every day. And you'd feel yet more stress and disappointment when the markets fall, as they always do, sooner or later.

When markets do fall, you'd be even more worried. Naturally, you'd be tempted to try and protect your money, so you might switch out of equity based investments into something safe. By then you'd be too late, of course. Your money will already have gone down! Then, when you feel confident the market has recovered, you'd reinvest. But again, it's all too late! Selling low, buying high, this is a sure fire way to devastate wealth.

Worse though, what about your precious time on this wonderful planet?

If you didn't know you had 'Enough' you'd probably let opportunities pass you by. You wouldn't climb those mountains. You wouldn't sail those seas. You wouldn't DO STUFF while you have the chance.

Then, sadly, you'd eventually realise you'd become too old to enjoy yourself. Your knees gone ... your hips gone ... then you're in a wheelchair. And then ... you're dead.

Perhaps, you didn't live life to the full? Perhaps you didn't do stuff when you had the chance?

Perhaps you're lying on your death-bed, with all the money, but no time ... and then ... it's too late.

All this, because you didn't realise that you had ENOUGH!

There are millions of people who suffer from this problem. But you needn't be one of them.

The big question is: *'How much IS enough?'* How much do YOU really need for the rest of your life? What's YOUR Number?

In my 30 years as a Financial Planner, I've found there are only THREE types of people when it comes to financial planning. In the next few chapters we're going to take a look at these THREE types - and you can decide which one best applies to you.

Then you can work out, for you, how much is ENOUGH?

That's what this book is all about.

There is no 'perfect' answer, of course. But this book and supporting resources will help you get a much better understanding of where you are heading financially so that you can make better decisions, have a lot more peace of mind - and a lot more fun!

So, let's get started.

First though, I've got something really important to tell you. I need you to understand where I'm coming from and why I wanted to publish this book.

You'll see why it's important...

Chapter Two

A Smart Career Move?

Before we go any further, I'd better spill the beans.

I'm an 'Alternative' Financial Adviser.

Now, before your throw this book at the wall or burn it, I want you to notice the word *'Alternative'*.

Many years ago I noticed how 'Financial Advisers' were, for good reason, one of the least trusted professions.

So I saw an opportunity. I vowed to do the complete opposite to most advisers.

I decided to tell my clients the truth. It wasn't always what they wanted to hear, of course. But I told them anyway. I believed it was my job to do so.

Sadly, most Financial Advisers don't tell the truth. They're not lying as such. It's just that they're not telling you the truth. You'll see why over the next few chapters.

I've been a Financial Adviser since 1982. That's when I fell into financial services. I was 22.

I say 'fell' because that's exactly what happened. I never set out in life to be a financial adviser. Who on earth does!?

Back then, I was working as a trainee Quantity Surveyor, and I remember the day like it was yesterday.

It was a cold January day. I'd just got back to the office after being out on site since very early that morning. George Downes, my manager, a Geordie from Newcastle, came into my office all excited. He'd just received a new company car. He rushed me over to the window, pointed out into the frosty car park, and he said: *"Wey aye, man! Look at that! Canny net, that, like!"*

Then he said some magical words: *"Howay, man! If you work long and hard in this Company, one day, lad, one day, you might get one of those!"*

I think he was trying to inspire me.

It had the opposite effect.

He was pointing to his new, 1982 reg, sky blue, Vauxhall Cavalier.

Wow! Let me think that one through, George...

'… One day … if I work long and hard … in this Company … then … one day … I 'might' get one of those!'

He was 58. I was 22.

"One day?!" I thought! *"I want one of those NOW! Not when I'm 58!!"*

Thanks George. You did inspire me! To go out at lunchtime, get a newspaper, sit down with my sandwiches - and look for another job!

That's when I saw an enticing advertisement for a new career. It was in this thing called 'financial services', whatever that was?

Intrigued, I called the number in the ad.

The guy on the 'phone was very eloquent. I got an interview.

I put on my best suit - the one I'd got married in just a few months earlier - and off I went for my interview. It was in Bennett's Hill, Birmingham.

I got the job!

Don't be too impressed. Back then, anybody could become a Financial Adviser. All you had to do was pass the 'mirror test'.

Basically, it went something like this …

Ready...?

You were asked to breathe on a mirror. If it misted up, you got the job!

Ta da! I was now a Financial Consultant. More on that in a minute ...

First, I want to share something really, REALLY important.

By the way, the next couple of chapters are about me so you can miss these out if you want, and jump straight to the chapters concerning your money. But I feel compelled to tell you the following details about my own experiences. They carry an important message giving context to the 'money pages'.

Chapter Three

The Early Days

When I was growing up I hardly saw my Dad. He was always working.

He worked as a welder in a factory, working all the shifts he could. He worked days and he worked nights.

On top of that, when he wasn't working in the factory he was always doing odd jobs for people. He'd cut hedges, he'd mow lawns, he'd paint houses. He'd do anything he could to earn extra money so that he could provide for me, my mum and my three sisters.

All the time he'd be out there, working, working, working, so we could have a better life. I'm proud of my Dad.

When I was about fourteen, something happened between my Mum and Dad that I'll never forget.

It happened early one evening. My Dad had just got back from the factory. He'd changed out of his dirty boiler suit and into his gardening gear. He was half-way out of the door on his way to do yet another odd job. That's when my Mum said, with a sad look on her face: "*So ... what time will you be back for your 'tea', Derrick?*"

I think the word '*So ...*' must have hit a nerve.

I can still remember my Dad, raising his voice and replying to my Mum: *"I'm doing this for us, Mary!"* he said. *"I'm doing this for us! One day, when I've retired, then we'll have plenty of time to spend together, but right now I have to go to work!"*

And my Mum, trying her best to understand, said, "*Yes, yes, I know, Derrick.*"

Then, he was off. Gone to work. Again.

For thirty-five years or more, that's what Dad did. Always working; always *'doing it for us'* - and always for the right reasons you understand.

As you can imagine, when I was growing up, my hard-working Dad was my role model. He taught me his work ethic.

So ... guess what? I did odd jobs. I had three paper rounds. I cleaned windows. I cut hedges. I mowed lawns.

I painted houses. That's what you do when you have a Dad like mine.

I had money when my pals didn't. I had a mega record collection: Motown, Soul, Funk, Jazz & Blues. I bought my first car. All thanks to my Dad inspiring me to get out of bed in the morning and graft.

When I left school at 16, I became an apprentice carpenter. I worked hard at work and I worked hard in college. I won an 'Apprentice of the Year' award. My first success. My Mum was really proud.

Spurred on by my college success I paid for myself to go to college four nights a week, so I could eventually get off the tools and become a Quantity Surveyor.

You see, I'm a smart cookie! When I was working as a carpenter, I soon realised something about Quantity Surveyors. They all had company cars - and I wanted one!

So, I worked hard as a trainee Quantity Surveyor.

That brings me back to January 1982, when George got his new company car.

And I saw that ad ... and I became a 'Financial Consultant'.

So then, with my Dad's work ethic, I began to work hard as a financial adviser. Just like him, I worked days, I worked evenings. I worked weekends. I took work home.

I never stopped. I studied. I took exams. I got more and more qualified.

I paid the price to become 'successful'. I got good, really good. I was earning a great living. Following in Dad's footsteps, working hard as could be and providing for my young family.

But I was busy.

Busy. Busy. Busy.

Then I plucked up courage and ventured out on my own and started my own financial advice business. And I got even busier!

My business then took over my life. It was growing. So I'd work even later. I'd miss my children's school concerts - and other stuff too.

Worse, I'd be at home playing with my children, but I was often distracted. I was at home, but I wasn't really there. You see, my head was always somewhere else. My head was still full of work stuff!

Has this ever happened to you?

Ever noticed how easy it is to miss those precious moments because your head is somewhere else?

That's what happens when you get busy.

And then, suddenly, it happened …

Chapter Four

It Happened On A Thursday

It was a Thursday. Dad was hard at work when the telephone call came through. The factory manager tapped him on the shoulder and said: *"Derrick! You'd better get back home fast, something's happened to Mary!"*

He dropped everything. He rushed out of the factory and jumped into his car.

But sadly, by the time my Dad had raced the three miles to get home, it was too late.

His wife - my Mum - was dead. Aged 59.

Gone.

My Mum was the first person who mattered in my life to die. It knocked me for six.

But my grief? That was nothing compared to my Dad's.

His world fell apart. He'd lost the only woman he'd ever loved. It tore him to pieces.

He's eighty-six now. And to this day he still misses my Mum. He still lives his life full of regret. My Dad lives a life full of *"If only …?"*

"If only I'd spent more time with your Mum" he says, *"If only I'd been there for her"*, *"She loved her flowers, if only I'd bought her more flowers…"*

"If only …", *"If only …" "If only …"*

But, it's too late.

In fact, just the other day he said to me: *"Do you remember when you were little, how you'd say "Daddy, please will you play with me… please?" and I'd say "Sorry, but I've got to go to work". Do you remember that?"*

Damn right I remember it!

My Dad had never spoken to me about that before.

Then, with a tear in his eye, he said: *"I wished I'd played with you more often… I wish I'd taken you to watch the football, to see the Wolves play… I wish I'd gone fishing with you like you wanted!"*

Ouch! That hurt.

But he never did, you see. Because he was always working. For all the right reasons you understand. He was living his life the best way he knew how.

Yes. I'm really proud of my Dad.

Here's the thing …

Mum's death? It was my wake up call.

My Mum's death made me have a long hard look in the mirror. I suddenly realised - back in 1989 - that it was now me who was working all the hours I could. It was me who was running around like a busy fool. I was the guy who wasn't spending enough time with his family!

Suddenly it dawned on me …

… I was making exactly the same mistake as my Dad!

The financial rewards were different, yes. But I was making exactly the same mistake! Work! Work! Work!

That's when I decided to change things.

That's when I decided NEVER to work another evening, ever!

That's when I woke up!

My Mum's dying woke me up to the one Universal truth:

LIFE IS NOT A REHEARSAL!

Have you noticed? The older you get the more it feels like time is speeding up? It's scary. We only have so long on this beautiful planet, we have to make the most of each and every minute. We have to make sure we do the things we want to do in the small amount of time we've got left!

That's when I decided to be lazier and crazier than I've ever been before! That's when I decided to start booking time off BEFORE I booked time on.

But something more important happened …

A few weeks after my Mum died, I had my first appointment with a prospective new client.

Suddenly, in an instant, I found my purpose! I found my 'WHY'!

I found my reason for being a Financial Adviser …

Chapter Five

The Penny Drops. Thanks Mum.

I guess, for the first eight years of my life in financial services, I was like most other financial advisers.

I was busy selling financial products. Whizzing around: seeing one client after the next. Mortgages, pensions, investments, savings plans, life insurance ... you get the picture.

I can't say I was proud of myself. In fact, I was always a little embarrassed to call myself a 'Financial Adviser'.

If you want to have some fun, you try it! If someone asks what you do in any social situation, just say you're a Financial Adviser! I promise you, it's the easiest way to clear a room!

But then something happened to change my opinion of my role in life.

A few weeks after Mum died, when I finally plucked up enough enthusiasm to face a potential new client, something weird but rather magical then happened.

Bob and Sandra were both in their early 60's and approaching retirement. I was enjoying a really interesting first meeting with them. It felt good to be back in client meetings. They told me all about themselves; about their work, about their family, their interests, their hobbies.

I asked them what plans they had for their future.

Bob said: *"Well, one day we'd like to go trekking in New Zealand, ... and one day we'd like to climb Machu Picchu. And, you know what Paul, we've often both talked about learning to sail and one day buying a boat ..."*

"Yes," Sandra added *"... one day we'd like to cruise the Mediterranean!"*

That's when it happened.

Suddenly, without thinking, I blurted out: *"What was that you both said?"*

They looked at me, shocked.

"What was that you both said?" I exclaimed raising my voice even higher!

"You both said "One day!!!!"

"One day!!!!" I said, almost slamming the table. *"WHAT MAKES YOU THINK THERE WILL BE A 'ONE DAY'?"*

To this day I'm not sure what caused me to be so forceful. But in that meeting, perhaps spurred on by the loss of my dear Mum, I got a bit emotional. Something made me challenge what Bob and Sandra were saying.

"What do you mean by one day?" I said. *"Why not do these things NOW? Why not book these trips NOW, before it's too late? You're not getting any younger! Life's not a rehearsal, why not do it NOW?!!!"*

It went quiet.

He looked at her. She looked at him.

Had I blown it?

They looked at each other again, in silence.

What had I done? How rude had I been?

Feeling somewhat embarrassed, I apologised for my outburst.

I thought I'd better explain...

So I told them about the recent loss of my Mum, and how I'd already noticed my Dad living a life of terrible regret.

I shared with them how I remembered my Dad always saying to my Mum *"One day …"* But, for my Mum and my Dad, there was never going to be a *'One day'!*

I explained that my Dad would give ANYTHING to be in their position. They had each other. They had money. They had choices. They had time.

Sadly, my Dad had none of these things.

They were moved.

That's when they surprised me. Bob said: *"You know what Paul? … You are absolutely right!"*

They both then admitted how they had been going through their lives, always putting things off, always working too hard, not spending enough time together. Always saying *"One day …"*

Bob confessed, *"It's crazy, … we've been acting like we have forever! But we don't!"*

Then I had turned up in their life. They said it seemed like I was there for a reason… to *give them a good shake!*

Bob and Sandra both looked at me and said: *"But, Paul, it's all very well you saying: "Book it now!" and "Do these things now", but … really … can we afford to do these things now?!"*

Luckily, I'd just invested in some comprehensive financial planning software that could help me crunch all the numbers. Although I didn't realise it at the time, this software would help to change the lives of my clients.

It would give me the all important answers to this question! In other words, it would answer the one big question that everybody has: *'How much is ENOUGH?'*

After working with their financial information, and putting it all through my new software, the eventual answer for Bob and Sandra was: *"Yes! You can do all these things now - and, on really prudent assumptions, you'll never run out of money!"*

I can tell you, that changed Bob and Sandra's life.

They both quit their stressful jobs and retired early. They got on with the business of living life to the full - because now they knew they could!

But something more important had happened in that meeting.

Something so incredibly important ...

The penny had dropped ... for ME!

Suddenly, I realised that I had engaged with these clients on a whole different level. We hadn't talked about normal 'boring financial adviser stuff' (pensions, investments, etc).

Instead, with just a little bit of help from my Mum and Dad, we had focused on something far more important!

You see, I'd connected with them about something they could not deny. In fact, the ONE undeniable fact that nobody can deny!

LIFE IS NOT A REHEARSAL!!!

Bob and Sandra knew, deep down, that life is NOT a rehearsal. They knew that their precious time was slipping away!

Just like you, reading this. Deep down, YOU know this to be true.

Life is NOT a rehearsal. Precious time IS slipping away!

Suddenly, as if by magic, my service proposition had changed.

I realised in that meeting, because of my change in focus, we were all on the same team!

I was no longer on the opposite side, trying to sell Bob and Sandra some financial product on behalf of the financial services industry. Instead, we were all on the same side.

It was me and them. Together. Me helping them, inspiring them, cajoling them, challenging them to live their dreams now, before it's too late. Reminding them about this looming thing called 'old age' - the time when you become too old to enjoy yourself.

That's when the penny dropped!

That's when I realised the power and purpose of proper financial planning.

From that moment I embraced the fact that my job as a Financial Adviser was to help clients to GET and KEEP the life they want. To motivate people to do the things that inspire them. To do the things that they have always wanted to do. Most importantly, to do all these things before it's too late. It was my job, to help clients identify, achieve and maintain their desired lifestyle - WHATEVER HAPPENS. I realised - that was my job!

I suddenly realised that clients don't really want financial products or investments. They never have and never will.

They want the peace of mind and security of knowing where they're heading financially - and knowing what they need to do to secure their desired lifestyle.

When you think about it, apart from good health, 'lifestyle' is the only thing that anybody wants. It's what they've worked hard for. It's what they want to keep.

Of course, lifestyle is different for everybody. Some have a big lifestyle. Some have a little lifestyle. It's all about lifestyle.

Big lifestyle, big Number. Little lifestyle, little Number.

I knew there and then, that my job was to help clients understand 'how much is ENOUGH'. To help them discover their 'Number'. That 'Number' is the amount they need to keep living the life they want. Because once they understood their Number, I could help them to accumulate it, manage it, protect it and, most importantly, ENJOY IT! Before it's too late! That is PROPER financial planning.

I started to understand that regardless of what the financial services industry says (including the Financial Services Regulator), my job had little or nothing to do with financial products. These are just *'tools in the bag'*, used - if and when required - to get the job done.

I started to acknowledge how the Financial Services 'Industry' dominates the minds of Advisers everywhere, so that they conveniently keep focusing on selling the Industry's products and investments. That's how the Industry gets rich. But clients don't.

I became more and more aware of what I started to call 'financial porn': the excessive advertising of mostly expensive and often unnecessary financial products and investments to gullible Advisers - and to an unwary public.

These were the awakenings I experienced in the early Nineties. That's when I decided, there and then, to deliver just ONE service - to ALL clients.

I called this service *'Lifestyle Financial Planning'*: helping clients to identify, achieve and maintain their desired lifestyle - whatever happens. Armed with brilliant 'number crunching' software and the right mindset, I realised I could help any client, anywhere.

More importantly, from that moment forward, my confidence increased. I became more congruent. More authentic. I knew exactly what EVERY client wanted - and I knew how I could help them get it.

I also recognised that I had to walk the talk. I had to plan my own life first.

So I stopped being a busy fool.

I got good at delivering Lifestyle Financial Planning. Really good. This enabled me to achieve my own lifestyle goal. I semi-retired aged 45 and started sailing my yacht *'Spellbound'* around the world. Life is too short.

Seeing what happened to my Dad after the death of my Mum made me vow to live my life differently. For the last ten years I've spent six months working and six months sailing with my soulmate, Lynn. We spend precious time together because you never know when your time will be up. I'm confident my Mum would endorse my decision.

I don't say any of this to impress you. I say it to impress on you that life is NOT a rehearsal. Precious time IS slipping away.

Since I semi retired, I've been helping other Financial Advisers to STOP being 'Financial Advisers'! Instead, I've helped thousands of them to become professional Financial Planners. More specifically, I've been training them how to become *'Lifestyle Financial Planners'* so they can help their clients to live a great life without fear of running out of money, or dying with too much.

Over the last ten years I've had a ball. I've spoken to audiences of Advisers all over the world. I know, from the testimonials I receive, that I've helped them change the lives of thousands of their clients who now understand 'How much is ENOUGH?'

All thanks to my Mum!

But there's a problem. And that's why I've written this book.

There are some fantastic Financial Planners out there (many of whom I've trained) who put their clients at the forefront of everything they do. Their focus is firmly on helping their clients understand how much is ENOUGH and helping them to live life to the full with lifestyle financial planning.

But unfortunately … the majority of Advisers still don't get it!

Sadly, the majority of Financial Advisers only want to focus on peddling financial products and investments so they can earn their commission - or accumulate their 'assets under management' so they can rake off their fees. Sadly, they still work on behalf of the Industry.

They have no interest in telling their clients what I call 'The Truth About Money'.

So, out of immense frustration, I decided to write this book in the hope that I can help impact more lives by helping more people learn: 'How much is ENOUGH'.

Let's see how all this applies to you.

Chapter Six

What Are You Waiting For?

We all know that precious time is slipping away. The trouble is, because we're 'busy, busy, busy,' we tend to forget. We end up paying lip service to the fact that life is not a rehearsal.

So let's up the ante.

I'm quietly confident that what follows will sound familiar to you ...

Have you ever been on holiday for a fortnight? Of course you have!

Let's say you're going on holiday for two weeks, Saturday to Saturday. You know what it's like. You leave your house early in the morning and the whole of your first Saturday is spent travelling. You eventually arrive at your hotel. It's late, you're tired - you can't wait to hit the sack.

You know the feeling?

Next morning you wake up … in a strange place.

Firstly you think: *"Where am I?"*…

Then you realise!

"Hey, hey! I'm on holiday! I've got TWO WHOLE WEEKS to enjoy myself! I'm going to have so much fun. I'm going to do 'this', I'm going to do 'that'! Fantastic!" And off you go to start enjoying yourself. You've earned it!

Then, after a few days, it's Wednesday of the first week. By now you are well and truly settled in. You know your way around your hotel. You're in the groove!

You think to yourself: *"This is brilliant! It feels like I've been here for ages … but it's only Wednesday! I've still got another week and a half left of this! Fantastic!"* and off you go to have even more fun.

Then, after a few more days that seem to go on forever, it's Saturday - the start of your second week. And then you think: *"Hey! That first week was great! And I've still got another week left of this! Fantastic!"*

But then, suddenly, in what seems like a blink of an eye … you're checking in at the airport …. and you're on your way home!

Have you ever felt like this?

What happens to that second week!!!?

Has this ever happened to you? It's certainly happened to me! And it's happened to hundreds of people I've shared this story with.

Here's my point ...

Are you over the age of 40 or 45?

Guess what?

You're already into your second week!

It's speeding up fast, isn't it?

Your life is speeding up!

It's a fact. The older we get, the faster time seems to slip by.

As I write this, it's 2016! All the fuss and celebrations surrounding the Millennium seem like only a short time ago. Freddie Mercury died, when? Princess Diana? When? 9/11, was when? All seem like 'not long ago'.

My kids? It only seems like five minutes ago that they were toddlers. Now look at them!

I'm now in my late fifties! (Gulp! Typing that just doesn't feel right!)

Yet, it feels like only yesterday when I was sat on a bench down at the park with my best pal, Pete. I was in my Wolves strip and Pete was in his Aston Villa kit. We were just kids.

For some reason, we were trying to work out what year it would be when we would hit 50! It would be 2009! How we laughed! It seemed so far off! We just couldn't believe it! 2009!

And then... 'BOOM'!

Fifty? That's now several years ago!!

Now, I'm a lot closer to 60 than I am 50! Yet 50 seems like 5 minutes ago!

Precious time IS slipping away. You know it. I know it. Before long, you and me, we might be in a wheelchair or in a Nursing Home. It will be too late - and then we'll be dead.

Sorry to put the screws on you - but someone has to!

Therefore, what is it that YOU want to do BEFORE IT'S TOO LATE?

What do you want to do before you're dead in a box?

What needs to happen for you to have had a life well lived?

As Mark Twain said: *"Twenty years from now you will be more disappointed by the things you didn't do than by the things you did do"*.

We all know this to be true. But we get caught in the *"if, when, then"* trap. *"When I have more money..."*, *"When the kids grow up..."*, *"When I have more time..."* *"When I've retired...* " - then it's too late, and we're dead in a box with our name on it!

Life is for living! Yet both you and I have seen way too many people die, or succumb to illness, without having experienced life to the full.

This book is about waking up to the inevitable fact that we are here for the blink of an eye. It's not about being the wealthiest man/woman in the graveyard. It IS about lying on your deathbed with a mischievous grin on your face, while you giggle to yourself: *"That was so much fun!"*

This book will help you to do just that.

We're going to take a look at the THREE types of people I've come across in my time as a Lifestyle Financial Planner. You can then decide which most applies to you and plan accordingly.

But first, I want to share a simple idea with you that could completely change the way you look at your money and how you see your financial future. It's my bucket analogy.

Let's get stuck in.

Chapter Seven

Understanding Your Bucket

I hope you understand why I needed to share my story with you in the earlier chapters. Hopefully, you will now understand that it's not all about the money. It's about your life, and what you want to do with the time you have left on this planet.

In this chapter I want to show you a simple idea that I have been presenting to clients for twenty years or more. It really helps them to understand their money. In fact, this simple concept has changed many lives.

If you can get to grips with this basic idea you really will know more about financial planning than most financial advisers!

What I'd like you to do now is to imagine a simple bucket. Let me draw one for you, here you go:

We've all got a bucket. This is YOUR bucket.

Now, inside your bucket you have some money:

But - and this is really important - the ONLY money we can include inside your bucket is LIQUID money. It must be easily accessible, readily realisable money: bank savings, deposits, cash, the cash value ISAs, of shares, unit trusts, investment bonds, etc.

You see, here's the thing about money inside your bucket: you must be able to get at it! It has to be accessible. You must be able to lay your hands on it whenever you want, normally within 7-10 days.

In other words, it's YOUR money - you can spend it whenever you like. And that is why money inside your bucket is very important money!

OK? Got that?

So, pretty simple so far.

Now, you've most probably got other assets that you've accumulated over the years. For example, you might own a house. In fact, your home could be your most valuable asset.

But, you've guessed ... your home is NOT inside your bucket!

Your house sits up here, outside of your bucket, for one simple reason: it's tied up money. You can't spend it.

You can't take a door knob off your front door and pay your food bill with it at the supermarket!

For many people, although their house is an asset, it's also a liability - perhaps with a mortgage to pay, utility bills, running costs, maintenance etc.

Of course, one day in the future you might decide to downscale your house and move somewhere smaller and less expensive. Like so:

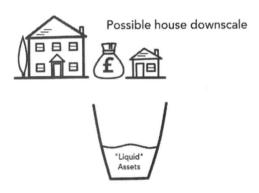

At that point, any difference in value between your current house and your next house will then become 'liquid' and fall into your bucket, like so:

So, at some future date, a house downscale might top up your bucket.

Are you with me so far?

This could obviously help your financial plan immensely which we'll see in future pages.

Your Pension Funds

Another big asset outside your bucket could be your pension funds. Here you go:

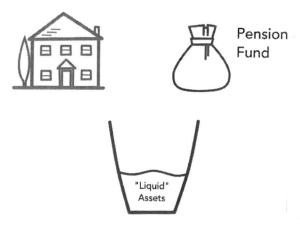

Pension Fund

"Liquid" Assets

Up until recently (in the UK) it's been called *'your pension fund'* but it's never really been your money. You could never access that money to spend how you wish.

The good news is (in the UK) once you are over 55, you can now access your pension fund pretty much however you see fit, (subject to a tax deduction). This flexibility has applied in other countries, such as the US and Australia, for some years, whereas in other countries flexible access to your pension is still not an option.

The thing to remember though, is this: your pension fund is OUTSIDE of your bucket UNTIL you take chunks of it (or draw income) into your bucket.

For example, at retirement you might take a tax free lump sum from your pension and then draw an income from your pension fund which then flows into your bucket, like so:

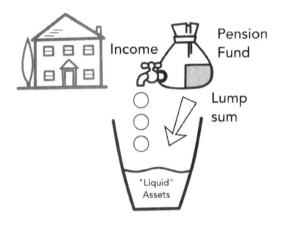

OTHER ASSETS

You might also have other assets outside of your bucket, such as a second property etc.

If you are a business owner, you might have the value of your business, or the value of your shares in your business. Again this sits outside of your bucket, like so:

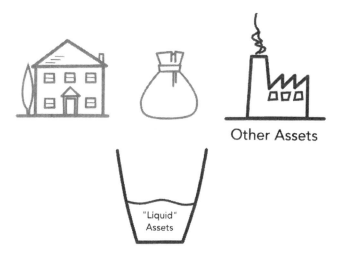

Other Assets

"Liquid" Assets

Obviously your business (if you have one) could be valuable. But until you sell it you can't spend it. So it has to stay outside of your bucket until it is sold. At which point, that sale value will then come into your bucket.

This applies to any other 'non liquid' assets: second properties, etc.

If you own a business please read: 'A Special Note For Small Business Owners' in Chapter Twenty for a more detailed analysis on this topic.

The important thing to remember about assets outside of your bucket is this: although this is your money, you can't spend this money until you sell those assets. That's why they have to be treated differently in the context of your financial planning.

To summarise so far; you have money INSIDE YOUR BUCKET which is yours, you can spend it whenever you like. You have other money/assets OUTSIDE of your bucket, which, although it's your money, you can't spend the latter until you sell those assets.

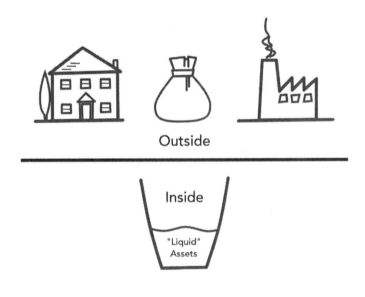

CURRENT INFLOWS

OK?

Let's now move on to CURRENT INFLOWS into your bucket.

If you're still working, you will have a salary or earned income for yourself and/or your partner coming into your bucket.

These CURRENT incomes are flowing into your bucket (on the right).

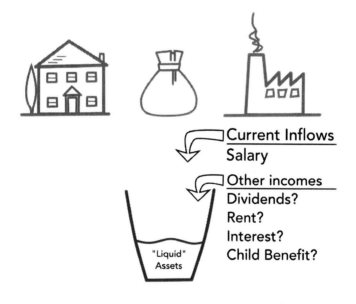

You might have other income as shown. For example, if you run your own business you might pay yourself dividends from your business. Or you might have young children and receive child benefit.

Interest on savings, income from Buy to Let properties or maintenance payments from an ex-partner are other examples. (You'll know what your current inflows are, but if not, don't worry. I'll help you identify these later).

The chances are (certainly if you are still working) that all these inflows are temporary. In other words they are going to stop one day. For instance, your salary might stop when you retire. If you have a business, your dividends or share of profit will stop when you sell or close down your business. So these are temporary inflows.

The good news is, at various stages of your life, other inflows will start.

FUTURE INFLOWS.

In the future other 'inflows' might start:

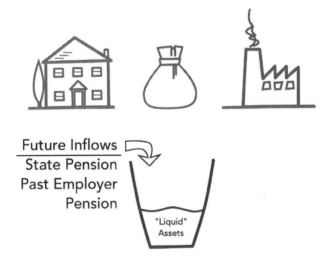

~ 56 ~

For example you might start to receive a State Pension at State Retirement Age (for yourself and / or your partner); you might also receive a pension from a current or past employer.

As I mentioned earlier, at some future date, you MIGHT downscale your house, in which case a lump sum will be added to your bucket like so:

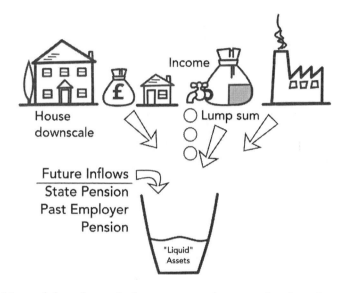

You might take cash from your retirement fund or draw an income, as shown.

If you have a business, you MIGHT sell that business.

I say 'MIGHT' sell your business because selling your business is probably the one thing you can't control.

So, it all looks pretty good so far, don't you think?

You see, on this basis your bucket should just fill up, and up, and up!

Like so:

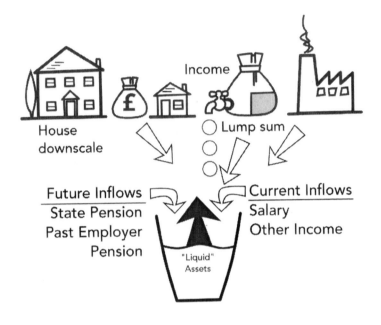

The only trouble is; this doesn't happen.

YOUR EXPENDITURE REQUIREMENTS

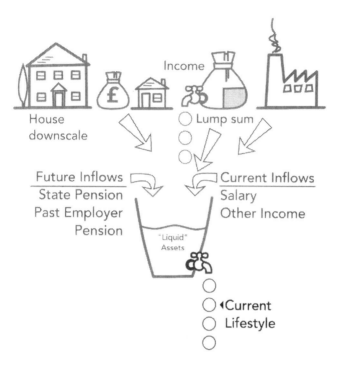

At the bottom of your bucket, you've got some TAPs.

This FIRST tap is effectively the cost of your CURRENT lifestyle.

This is the cost of you living the life you currently choose to live. To illustrate: it's the cost of you running your BMW convertible, your partner's Range Rover Vogue. It's the cost of educating your children privately, the cost of your weekend breaks, your annual skiing trip and your holiday in the Seychelles ... you get the picture?

In other words, however you live your life, there's a cost to it, and that's what is draining money from your bucket.

Now you might not drive a BMW Convertible or a Range Rover Vogue, and you might not take your holidays in the Seychelles. This was just an example. Everybody is different. We need to personalise this to your situation which we will do in a few pages time.

Don't worry about that for now.

Remember! It's important to live a good life now! Life is not a rehearsal!

Here's the thing ...

One day, this first 'current lifestyle' tap will get turned off. This will be when you reach your chosen retirement age. At this point a different tap gets turned on - YOUR SECOND TAP.

YOUR ACTIVE RETIREMENT TAP

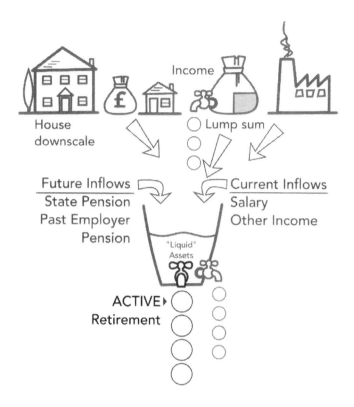

This is your 'active retirement tap' - the cost of you living a good life in retirement. (Remember, that's the plan!)

This will include the cost of the things you want to do when you retire - while you are still young enough to do so!

For example, you might want to travel more? You might want to go trekking in the Himalayas? You might want to learn to fly? You might want to go on more cruises?

You might want more meals out? More city breaks? Or more walks down to the pub?

You will probably want to do lots of things you never had time to do when you were working.

Here's the thing: whatever you want to do - big things or small things - there's probably a cost to it.

In fact, it may even be that at this stage of your life you would like to spend more money than you ever did before!

Why?

Because now you've got all the time in the world to enjoy yourself! And so you should! Life's not a rehearsal remember!

YOUR LATE RETIREMENT TAP

Time flies when you're having fun. So, sadly, there will come a time when your 'active retirement tap' gets turned off and a different tap opens.

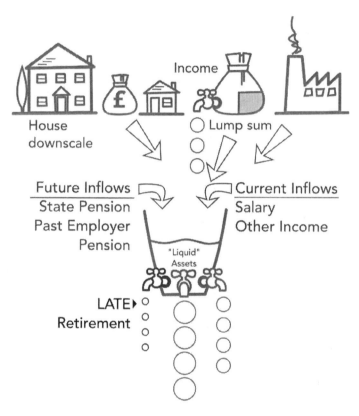

This is the stage of your life when you become, what I call, *'too old to enjoy yourself'*.

It's the time in your life when you just can't 'do stuff' anymore. Your knees might have gone. Your hips might have gone. Your hearing may be impaired. You're worn out. You're knackered!

In fact, if you're anything like me, it's starting to happen already! I've always tried to keep fit. But now I just can't do the things I used to do. I might try some physical pursuit that I could easily do 10 years ago, but now, when I do, I'm stiff as a board and can't walk for 3 weeks afterwards!

It's a stark reminder that becoming *'too old to enjoy yourself'* is inevitable. It's on its way. When you reach this stage of later life you you'll have trouble getting up the stairs, never mind getting up a mountain. You'll find it hard to get in and out of a wheelchair, never mind in and out of a yacht! You get the picture? It happens to us all, sooner or later.

At this stage of your life your needs WILL change. Now you'll want peace of mind and security.

It could be you'll now spend a lot less money. The time for having F-U-N will have probably gone. Of course, it is highly likely that now other costs may arise, like health and long term care fees.

This is the stage of your life when you definitely don't want to be worrying about money. And there's no need to, if you plan ahead using the ideas in this book.

AND THEN YOU'RE DEAD!

Then, sadly, you end up in a box with your name on it.
You're dead!

Like so:

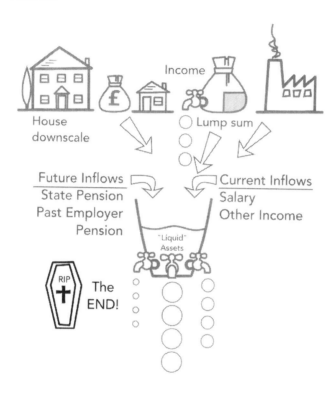

A full bucket will be of little use to you now, don't you
agree?

We'll discuss other reasons why you shouldn't die with a
full bucket later on.

Now, there is one other additional tap that you might need to turn on and off from time to time, and that's what I call a 'One Off' tap.

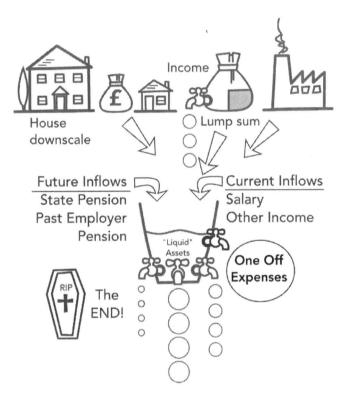

This additional tap (on the right) is for 'one off' expenses that need to be paid for from time to time. It could be the cost of a child's wedding? It could be the one off cost of a special holiday or world cruise? It could be the purchase of a brand new motor home? In other words, this tap is for 'one off' events that occur at various stages of your life that could seriously impact your bucket.

You get the idea?

So, just to summarise ...

You've got money inside your bucket - you can spend this money whenever you want.

You've got money outside of your bucket which you can only spend when you sell those assets.

You've got money coming into your bucket now (current inflows) which one day might stop.

You've got future inflows that one day might start coming into your bucket.

And, of course, you've got your three stages of expenditure - your three main taps:

1) NOW, your current lifestyle tap. Your expenditure needs before retirement (assuming you're still working).
2) Your 'active retirement' tap, when you want to have the most fun - while you are still fit and able to do so.
3) Your later retirement tap - when you start to become less active and 'too old to enjoy yourself' ...

Plus, you've also got:

4) Your occasional 'one off expenses' tap - for 'one off' items that need to be allowed for.

Make sense so far?

So, here's the really big question ...

Chapter Eight

What's Going To Happen To YOUR Bucket?

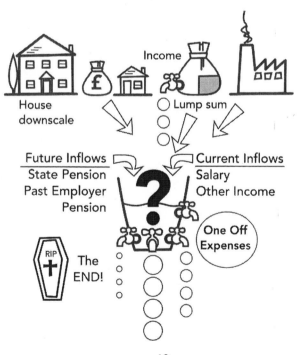

House downscale

Income

Lump sum

Future Inflows
State Pension
Past Employer
Pension

Current Inflows
Salary
Other Income

One Off Expenses

RIP

The END!

From a financial planning point of view, what's going to happen to your bucket is really the only thing that matters.

Never mind the detail about which investment you should choose? Or which deposit account is best? Or which ISA? None of that really matters.

What matters most is ... what's going to happen to your bucket?!

I can tell you now; one of TWO things is likely to happen.

Either:

1) Your bucket is going to run out.

In other words, there's not enough money in your bucket now or in the future to support the cost of your desired lifestyle.

What this means is, when the money runs out, your future lifestyle taps will have to be turned down - or turned off! Which means one thing: that you won't be able to continue to live the life you have become accustomed to.

That's not a good outcome! Why work for 30 or 40 years only to find out that your bucket is going to run out?!

Here's the GOOD NEWS! When you understand your bucket you can forecast what is likely to happen. You can start to exercise control over how full that bucket needs to be. You can prevent your bucket from ever running out. More on this later.

2) The next thing that can happen to your bucket ... is probably worse!

Instead of running out, your bucket could fill up and up and up! It NEVER runs out.

This means that you eventually go to your grave ... with TOO MUCH money!

Why is this worse?

Let me explain.

If you go to your grave with too much money in your bucket, here's what's probably going to happen.

No doubt, you will have paid tax throughout your whole life. Income Tax and National Insurance on everything you've ever earned; Value Added Tax (VAT) on pretty well everything you've ever spent; you pay tax on your capital gains; tax when you buy or move house (Stamp Duty) and tax when you fill up your car with fuel! You even pay tax on your booze!!

Think about it, throughout your life you've paid tax, tax, TAX!

So, to go to your grave with TOO MUCH money in your bucket and risk paying **your biggest tax bill ever** is crazy, don't you think?

I'm talking here about ESTATE TAXES due on death! (Up to 40% tax of your estate in the UK).

Surely, you've paid enough tax already! To go to your grave with too much money and lose a large chunk of your hard earned wealth to the tax man - which is tax on money that you've already paid tax on - is madness.

But that's exactly what is happening to an increasing number of people who don't understand what's going to happen to their bucket. In other words, they don't know how much is ENOUGH!

The good news is, once you understand the concept of the bucket, you can make planning your future a lot easier. You can PLAN to avoid 'dying with TOO MUCH'.

In fact, understanding your bucket could save you and your family hundreds of thousands in unnecessary tax!

But there's something I haven't told you ...

There is something far worse about dying with too much.

It's not the tax!

No. It's something far, far worse.

If you go to your grave with too much money it probably means one thing ...

You didn't do stuff!

You didn't enjoy your money when you could easily have afforded to do so!

Imagine, lying on your death bed, with all that money - but NO MORE TIME!

Then, you realise ... that you didn't do things!

You didn't climb those mountains.! You didn't sail those seas! Perhaps you worked more than you needed to! Perhaps you worked 'til 65 when you could easily have retired at 55! Imagine that! You were working when you could have been playing! You didn't have that dream trip on the Orient Express with the love of your life before they died! You didn't help your children out when they really needed it most! And then, there you are, on your death bed, with all that money - but no time!

And the Tax Man is lurking...

And you're thinking... *"@&@*!! @&@*!!! @&@*!! <insert your preferred expletive here!>"!!!*

You'd probably be thinking *"I wish I'd known this was going to happen! I'd have done more 'stuff'! I'd have lived more! I'd have been less stressed about money! I'd have given more! I'd have gone First Class!"*

But, it's too late!

Well, that's what this book is all about: making sure that this doesn't happen to you.

(Sorry to be so dramatic - and repetitive - but you get the point?!)

You need to know what's going to happen to your bucket! **So you can enjoy your money!** So you can have peace of mind about where you are heading financially.

Again, here's the good news ...

Now I've got you thinking about it, we can do something about it.

I'm soon going to help you work out what's going to happen to YOUR bucket.

Let's now take a look at the three types of people and the challenges they face. Then we can see which one best applies to you.

Chapter Nine

Which Money Type Are You?

In my thirty years as a Lifestyle Financial Planner, dealing with clients from all backgrounds, with various levels of wealth, I've only ever come across THREE types of clients: just three.

These are:

Type 1) *'Not Enough'* type clients - their bucket is going to run out.

Type 2) *'Got Too Much'* type clients - their bucket is going to overflow.

and

Type 3) *'Just Rights'!* These have just the right amount - but the only trouble is, they might not realise it!

Let's take a look at each of these and get a feel for the problems they face. I'll also be including a couple of real life Case Studies, which I hope you'll find useful.

But I want you to promise me something...

When you read these case studies, please forget about the amounts of money involved.

It's easy to think *"That doesn't apply to me, I don't have that much money!"* Or *"I have much more money than that! This doesn't apply to me!!"* It's the principle I want to get across.

I promise you, no matter how much money you have, or don't have, you WILL fall into one of these three camps.

Let's find out ...

Chapter Ten

The 'Not Enough's'

As the name suggests, these are people who haven't yet got enough money to last their whole life through. Their bucket is most definitely going to run out. More often, they are people who will NEVER have enough UNLESS they start accumulating wealth. They need desperately to know how much is ENOUGH.

Solving their problem is not as complicated as you might think. In simple terms, they probably need to increase the inflows going into their bucket OR they need to consider reducing the outflows going out of their bucket (expenditure / lifestyle) now or in the future.

It's no crime!

It's no crime to be a *'Not Enough'*. If you think you might be a *'Not Enough'* type person you most certainly aren't alone. Millions of people are in this situation. It's not your fault. No one has ever helped you to understand how to financially plan your future. No one has ever helped you work out how much is ENOUGH! No one has ever explained to you about your bucket!

This is where I blame the Financial Services Industry including most Financial Advisers. The Industry has failed consumers - its only real interest is in selling financial products, when really it should be answering these much bigger questions.

One thing is for sure: the Government isn't going to look after you! They'll have you working until you drop!

The fact is, if you're currently a *'Not Enough'* type person, you're not going to be able to maintain your current lifestyle. It's as simple as that. Your taps are going to have to be turned down, or turned off. Unless YOU do something about it.

The good news is this: it's easy to do something about it and it needn't be painful. It just needs you to face up to some simple facts. Then, step by step, you can start doing something about it - so you accumulate ENOUGH! So that your bucket doesn't run out!

Or, it might mean facing up to some home truths and accepting that certain things are going to have to go, now or in the future.

Let's now take a quick look at an example of a *'Not Enough'* type client and how an understanding of what was going to happen to their bucket really helped them.

CASE STUDY 1

Mr & Mrs Not Enough

Steve and Sue worked hard. Very hard. But they played hard too: they enjoyed the lifestyle which they had worked hard to create for themselves and their daughters, Rebecca and Lucy.

Steve was 45 and he had a plan. It was his own financial plan. He wanted to retire at 55.

Steve hated three things:

> His mortgage.
> Pensions.
> And, most of all, financial advisers!

So Steve's plan was simple: pay off his mortgage as quickly as possible. Then, when he was mortgage free, he intended to accumulate as much as possible via his business between 45 and 55 – so that he could retire early.

Simple!

Steve didn't think he had a problem. He didn't need any 'advice'.

However, Steve's accountant recommended that Steve should speak with me.

At our meeting I spent some time getting to know Steve and Sue. I wanted to understand the life they'd had, the life they'd got, and the life they wanted in the future. I helped them to think about the lifestyle they desired throughout their life. I also wanted to understand why retirement at 55 was so important?

The reason?

It transpired that Steve wanted to 'escape' at age 55 and pursue his passion! His passion was Motor Sport. He loved it! He wanted to do a lot more of it while he was still young enough and, more importantly, fit enough to do so. He wanted to do more hill climbs, more rallying, some saloon car racing and Formula 3. Better still, both Steve and Sue wanted to travel the world together, ticking off more Formula One events. They wanted to 'do stuff' – *'before it's too late!'*

But for Steve, why 55? Why was that so important?

Steve shared with me the fact that his own father had worked hard his whole life, retiring at 65, only to drop down dead at age 67.

It turned out that this was Steve's main motivator. He could not bear the thought of that happening to him. More than anybody, Steve knew – and understood – that 'Life is NOT a rehearsal' and Steve lived it accordingly. That's why Steve worked so hard now, so he could 'escape' early.

With this knowledge, I said I would work with Steve and Sue through a lifestyle financial planning process to help them understand where they were heading financially.

I helped them to identify the cost of their current and future desired lifestyle. I built in the cost of continuing private education for Rebecca and Lucy. I built in the cost of their daughter's weddings. I encouraged Steve and Sue to really focus on the lifestyle they expected at various stages of their lives. We then put all of this into a simple expenditure questionnaire. I went back to my office and crunched the numbers.

Unfortunately, at our next meeting, I had to break the bad news.

I carefully explained (with the help of my financial planning software) that on agreed assumptions, Steve and Sue's current plan would see them running out of money early - by age 67! That's not a good plan.

Fortunately, with the help of my software, using meaningful, prudent assumptions, it was possible to help Steve and Sue to discover how much was ENOUGH. This would be the amount of money they needed by age 55 to ensure they could live the life they wanted – without fear of ever running out of money.

You've guessed it. Due to the cost of their current and future desired lifestyle it was a BIG NUMBER.

But once they understood 'How Much is ENOUGH' they realised immediately that they needed to do something about it. Better to know, than blindly head off into the future without knowing what was in store. I then worked with Steve and Sue to help find ways of accumulating the money through savings and investments. More importantly, I showed them how they could utilise their greatest asset (their business) to help build their Number.

Once Steve and Sue began to understand 'How Much is ENOUGH', an amazing thing started to happen. In their business, Steve started to see opportunities everywhere to increase turnover, reduce costs and create profit. All of which would help Steve and Sue to achieve their Number. The funny thing is, those opportunities were there all along! But Steve didn't need to see them - UNTIL HE KNEW HIS NUMBER!

Steve and Sue are now well on course to achieve their Number and achieve their intended retirement at age 55. Steve now has a reason to work hard; a real 'WHY'. Steve is motivated. Steve is inspired. Steve knows where he is going.

For the first time ever he could see his target. And now, as it gets closer, it becomes even easier to hit.

IN A NUTSHELL

When you know what you are aiming at it becomes easier to hit. Knowing your Number - How Much Is Enough - is the single most important thing you need to know when planning your future. **When you know what you are trying to achieve, miraculously, your mind starts coming up with ways of achieving it.**

Chapter Eleven

The 'Got Too Much'

These are people who have more than ENOUGH already, or are heading that way. Their bucket is definitely going to overflow. They are likely to go to their graves with way TOO MUCH money.

That sounds like a nice sort of problem. But it is a problem nonetheless!

Again, the answer is knowing how much is ENOUGH to last your whole life through. Then, if there's going to be a surplus - because you're a Got Too Much - it opens up a whole host of possibilities.

For example, we mentioned earlier that the biggest problem about being a Got Too Much is potentially becoming the richest man (or woman) in the graveyard. Nobody wants that. As they say, *"You can't take it with you"*.

So, once you know how much is ENOUGH, you can plan your life accordingly. In particular, you can SPEND MORE - and feel good about it!

A good reason to spend more is that you ain't coming back! THIS is it! Life is not a rehearsal. Now is your chance to do stuff, while you still can. It's no good being stuck in a wheelchair or in a nursing home wishing you had done more with your life when you had the chance.

Another good reason to spend now is that spending your money is one of the best ways of reducing your estate. This means it's a great way to avoid taxes on your death. If you spend more, you leave less for the tax man. Simple as that.

Or, perhaps you've done all you want with your life. You don't need or don't want to spend more. In which case, once you know your 'Number' - how much is ENOUGH - you can start to feel comfortable about giving money away.

Perhaps you could help your children or grandchildren - and feel really good about it. Why? Because you know it's OK to do so! Because you know it makes sense. Far better to pass on money now when you are alive so you can actually see the benefit it brings to those you help, rather than miss all that when you're dead and gone.

Of course, it's also an opportunity to help good causes: to leave a legacy. To do or create something that lives on after you're gone.

Again, it's all about knowing how much is ENOUGH - for YOU.

Here's another great thing. Once you understand that you are a Got Too Much, once you've worked out that you've got more than ENOUGH, you can do something rather wonderful - something that will bring you more peace of mind.

You can reduce risk!

It never fails to amaze me how so many people - who have more than enough money - still stress and worry about their money. More often than not, this is because they've got their money invested in all the wrong places! They often invest their money with a view of still trying to make MORE. But, when you think about it, for whose benefit is this, really? The Tax Man?

Once you realise that you are a Got Too Much, you can start thinking about investing for 'prudence', rather than 'performance'.

Let's now take a quick look at a typical Got Too Much type client ...

Remember, when you read these case studies, please forget about the amounts of money involved. It's the principle I want to get across.

CASE STUDY 2

Mr & Mrs 'Got Too Much'

John and Mary were in their late 60's and happily enjoying their retirement. And so they should!

John had worked long and hard in a Company that he had helped to grow over many years. He had benefited from his share options. He had accumulated some real wealth.

They had plenty of income in retirement: from his Final Salary pension, from some private pensions, interest from their savings and dividends from their shares and ISAs. They had accumulated a lot of money and they were enjoying it!

House-wise John and Mary were 'empty nesters' and were about to downscale to a smaller, more manageable property. Their three children had all moved out some time ago and their five bedroom house was now far too big for them. They had found an apartment overlooking John's Golf Club. It was perfect. Their downscale in house value would soon see over £600,000 going from bricks and mortar (outside their bucket) into savings (inside their bucket).

But what did all this mean? And what about Inheritance Tax?

John was encouraged to meet me by one of his golfing pals who was a client of mine.

As always, I spent some time really getting to know John and Mary. I enquired about the life they'd had and the life they'd got. I also wanted to fully understand what John and Mary had planned for their future. I also wanted to know if they had any plans to help their children and grandchildren. By asking these questions I helped them to identify the cost of the lifestyle they wanted to continue to enjoy – this gave a good indication of their 'expenditure' requirements throughout their life.

I also got them to think about what else they might like to do in their lifetime in order to really enjoy their remaining years. I gathered the facts about what they had accumulated; their capital position, their assets, their liabilities and their many sources of income. I also asked them to complete my expenditure questionnaire.

After returning to my office, and using my cutting edge financial planning software, together with a thorough understanding of their circumstances, I identified what was going to happen to their bucket.

This is what I found …

Based on the conservative assumptions they had made, after allowing for inflation, and after allowing for the potential costs of long term nursing care, John and Mary would NEVER, ever run out of money.

In fact, John and Mary's wealth would continue to increase, even after allowing for extra expenditure.

Instead of running out of money, John and Mary were well on course to die... with TOO MUCH!

This sounds like great news. It is great news! But this meant John and Mary had a big problem.

John had paid a huge amount of tax throughout his whole life. In fact, they were about to pay yet another slug of tax (£24,000 Stamp Duty) when they downscaled and moved to their new apartment.

Tax, tax, tax.

Unfortunately, unbeknown to them, their biggest tax bill was still lurking ...

I helped John and Mary realise the size of their problem, and even though they had three children, just who was going to be the single, largest beneficiary of their hard earned estate ... ?

The Chancellor!

If both John and Mary died, the Inheritance Tax bill was already well over £1.4million. Even on low growth assumptions, it was forecast to get far worse.

But it didn't have to be that way.

Again, using my financial planning software, using conservative assumptions, I helped John and Mary work out just how much more they could afford to spend each year, and how much they could confidently afford to pass on to their children NOW and over the next ten years - without fear of ever running out of money.

Effectively, I helped John and Mary create a 'spending and gifting programme'.

John and Mary are now well on course to eliminate their Inheritance Tax liability. They are on course to manage their money to give them the life they want whilst gradually passing on wealth down to their children and grandchildren so the Chancellor does not benefit.

They also booked a 'First Class' Round The World Cruise. And why not?

They can do this, because John and Mary now know – and more importantly, understand – just how much is ENOUGH.

IN A NUTSHELL

When you understand how much is ENOUGH you can enjoy your money and feel good about it. This is what I call REAL wealth management: managing your wealth to give you the life that you want. **Why have wealth if it doesn't give you the life that you want?**

Chapter Twelve

The Just Right's

So here's the third type of person. The 'Just Right'.

Many people have just the right amount of money for the rest of their life. But the only trouble is, they just don't know it!

The 'Just Right' type has no idea what's going to happen to their bucket. Because no one has ever shown them.

So they stress and they worry about money. They invest in all the wrong places. They take too much risk, which of course ruins their peace of mind and possibly erodes their capital.

You may be one of these people.

Have you ever considered: you might not be enjoying life as much as you could? You might be going without? Perhaps, saying 'no' when you could be saying 'yes'? You might have the heating on low in the winter and feel cold, when you could easily turn up the thermostat and be comfortable. You might buy cheap plonk instead of good wine. You might be taking one holiday a year when you could easily afford three. You might be missing out big time.

Or worse, because you don't know what your financial future looks like, (because you don't know what's going to happen to your bucket) you might spend your hard earned money but then regret it! Perhaps buying something then immediately wishing you hadn't. Again, that's no way to have fun!

Perhaps you are still working when you could be playing. Or perhaps you're saving when you should be spending!

Yet, through all this, you could already have ENOUGH. You might have the right amount of money to see you through.

There are millions of people in this situation. The 'financial porn', the newspapers, the money pages pray on folk like this. They want you to feel insecure. They want you to feel like you don't know enough, so you keep reading their scaremongering articles - all the time helping them make zillions out of advertising stuff at you.

Perhaps you're better off than you thought? Perhaps you're going to be OK? It's time to find out.

Here's the thing ...

If, on prudent assumptions, you knew you were going to be OK, you could relax. You could simplify things. You could de-risk. You could enjoy your money without feeling guilty. You could do more, you could live more.

Let's take a look at a couple of real life examples of the 'Just Rights' ...

CASE STUDY 3

Mr & Mrs Ten Years Younger

Graham and Pauline were in their late 50's, but looked and felt like they were in their 70's ...

Working 60 – 70 hours a week in their engineering business, their Sunday mornings were spent finishing off the week's paperwork. Like so many small business owners, their business was slowly killing them.

Holidays? They were few and far between.

Hobbies? None.

Stress? Lots.

It's a common problem.

After spending time getting to know them, I identified Graham and Pauline's real objective. This was to escape from their business and get on with their life!

Graham's ambition was to learn to fly ... 'before it's too late'.

I asked Graham why he had not yet learned to fly. He said that since the flying lesson bought as a 'birthday treat' - a gift from Pauline some ten years earlier - he had always put it off. Their business did not really allow any time off to take up such a time consuming hobby.

Furthermore, business pressures were always too much of a distraction to focus on something so intense as learning to fly. So, for ten years or more, it had remained just a dream. But, the trouble was, Graham wasn't getting any younger.

On talking further with Graham and Pauline it soon became apparent that substantial funds had been accumulated in various investments including ISAs and pensions etc. These had been ignored for many years and because no one had been meddling with their money it had performed quite well.

Through further discussion, I helped Graham and Pauline identify the cost of their current and desired future lifestyle, including the cost of flying lessons. I needed to understand this in order to calculate for them how much is ENOUGH – how much money they needed for the rest of their lives.

In the course of our discussions I asked about the chances of them selling their business. Graham and Pauline confirmed that an offer had recently been made for their business but they turned it down on the advice of their accountant. Their accountant had advised them that the £2million offered by the buyer was unacceptable and well below the £4-5 million of potential value that could be realised in the next 5-10 years.

So! That's why they were still working! That's why their business was slowly killing them! That's why Graham hadn't fulfilled his dream of learning to fly!

With my years of experience, I just knew something wasn't right. So I went back to my office and ran my calculations to find out what was going to happen to their bucket. Here's what I found …

Using prudent assumptions - and after 'stress testing' those assumptions - Graham & Pauline needed just an additional £500,000 to retire NOW, not in 3 year's time at aged 60!

If the cost of flying lessons and the purchase of a light aircraft was built in they needed just £750,000. NOW. And this was to start living the life they wanted NOW … not in 3 years time!

Trouble is, on the advice of their accountant, they'd recently turned down £2 million!

When they heard the news they were amazed. With my help and that of their accountant they eventually managed to get the deal back on the table and ended up selling their business for £1.8 million.

So, they escaped from their business. Graham learned to fly. And both he and Pauline continue to enjoy their retirement. Better still, they both now look – AND FEEL – 10 years younger!

IN A NUTSHELL

Some people already have ENOUGH. But they just don't realise it. Life's too short to spend it doing things that don't fulfil you.

CASE STUDY 4

Mr & Mrs Are We There Yet?

Mike and Sarah were nearly there, or so they thought. Trouble is they didn't know where 'there' was!

Mike was a Senior Pilot for a major airline. One night, flying at 35,000 feet over Outer Mongolia, out of nowhere a thought slipped into his mind: *"How much longer do I have to do this ...?"*

Increasing pressure, tighter regulations, continued testing, and regular cut backs - it was no longer the same. The fun had gone. And now, aged 55, he was thinking *'WHY am I still doing this?'*

What he really wanted to do was fly his own single engine, two-seater bi-plane. That was real flying. That was what he wanted - to buy and fly his own beauty.

He had a great pension. He'd built up some capital inside his bucket. He'd nearly paid off his mortgage. But what did it all mean? Was he 'there' yet? He needed help.

So he was recommended to see me to help him make sense of it all.

Firstly, I assisted Mike and Sarah to get a fix on what they wanted and when they wanted it - the sort of lifestyle they would enjoy. Travel? No thanks, not for them. They'd done enough of that! Now, their interest was in staying at home: Mike flying his bi-plane and Sarah breeding goats on their 20 acres of land.

I helped them to understand the cost of their desired future lifestyle. We identified what was inside their bucket, what was coming in (current and future inflows) and what was expected to be going out of their bucket (current and future expenditure requirements). I crunched the numbers to see how they fared.

Great news! On conservative assumptions, their bucket was just fine!

They'd already arrived - it's just they didn't realise it!

Immediate retirement was possible for Mike, so long as they downscaled to a smaller property in around twenty years at the age of 75-80.

So, knowing this, Mike gave up long haul and retired immediately. He now enjoys being at home with Sarah and the regular thrill of the wind in his face at the controls of his bi-plane - enjoying life on his own terms.

Sarah's goat population is coming along nicely too.

CASE STUDY 5

Mr & Mrs Do It Yourself

David and Elaine were living off the income from the capital they had accumulated over the years. After allowing for various pension incomes, David and Elaine were supplementing their income with interest and dividends from their savings. If interest rates went up they spent more. If interest rates went down they spent less.

Over the years they had accumulated a collection of ISAs and a portfolio of shares. Most of these had been purchased off the page from leading investment houses who tempted them with 'top performing funds' and 'promises' of high returns.

The trouble is, knowing when to buy investments is one thing, but knowing when to sell is another! Although they were too proud to admit it, over the years David and Elaine had gradually built for themselves a portfolio that they didn't really understand. It had become a big worry.

Every Sunday they wrestled with the money pages in the Sunday papers, and spent many hours wading through piles of Direct Mail, statements and valuations from their various investment providers.

So much bumph! What should they keep? What should they throw away? What should they ignore? What should they take seriously?

Now all of this wasn't too bad ... while their money was going up!

But when markets went down David and Elaine were really worried. So a friend of theirs suggested they ask me to look at their situation.

As usual I spent time getting to know them, about their present lifestyle, and their plans for the future. I asked about their hobbies and interests, their family, their goals, their hopes and dreams, their fears and worries.

That's when it became clear that their money was causing them sleepless nights.

I analysed their financial position, looked at all of their various investments, and scrutinised their income situation. I identified what was already inside their bucket and what was coming into their bucket now and in the future.

More importantly I got them to think about their expenditure requirements going forward and how much they would LIKE to spend to give them the life they wanted.

Then I used my software to help identify what was going to happen to their bucket.

Here's what I found ...

Based on conservative assumptions, their bucket was never going to run out.

They had TWO main options.

Their first option was to keep doing what they were doing - live off their fluctuating interest and dividends, forever worried about market movements, condemned to feel guilty about dipping into their savings whenever things got tight. Forever going without. Forever cutting back. Not living life to the full.

I showed them the consequences of this action. Using my software to illustrate what was going to happen to their bucket, they could see that their bucket would remain about the same. What this means is: they would die with too much money!

They'd never thought about it like this before.

I then showed them another option. The other option was to change their mindset and PLAN to spend their liquid capital in their lifetime. They could then leave the assets outside of their bucket - their home and personal effects - to their children when they eventually died - but they could enjoy spending the rest. This struck a chord. Even their children were saying that they wished their Mum and Dad would stop worrying and spend it!

So this 'bucket' exercise helped David and Elaine to understand just how much return they needed on their investments so their money inside their bucket lasted their lifetime.

This meant they could actually take LESS risk with their investments - and in the process consolidate and simplify their portfolio to reduce charges.

More importantly, David and Elaine got their life back.

No more wasting precious time stressing over the money pages every Sunday! Instead more fun, more eating out, more holidays, more treats for the grandchildren.

For David and Elaine, the bucket concept made their money make sense. They now knew the truth about money.

Let's now move on to the MOST important thing that drives your financial planning.

Chapter Thirteen

What's The One Thing Everybody Wants?

Over the last ten years, both in the UK and overseas, I've presented to thousands of leading financial advisers via various workshops, seminars or conferences. These are designed for advisers who have the good sense to want to move their businesses towards a client focused, fee based financial planning service. They are moving away from the commission driven, product focused sales based approach which has resulted in financial advisers NOT being the most trusted profession.

However, even when I ask a group of these cutting edge advisers what they think their clients really want, I'm astounded by the replies.

I'm often told that what they 'think' clients want is *'a trusting relationship with their adviser'* - and they want their adviser *'to be well qualified'* and *'to be experienced'*.

This is where I point out that surely these are not things that clients want. These are things clients EXPECT!

You expect your adviser to be well qualified don't you? You expect to be able to trust him or her? You expect to be given the right recommendations?

You don't say *"I always use this Doctor because he always gives me the right medicine!"* You EXPECT to be given the right medicine. And that's how it should be with financial advisers.

The good news is the financial advice 'industry' is gradually moving towards being a better qualified profession and over the next few years many of the poorly qualified, product sales based advisers will have left the industry. It's about time too.

Anyway, with a few more hints, Advisers eventually tell me what clients REALLY want. I'm then told it is: *'peace of mind', 'financial security'* and *'financial independence'.*

That's more like it don't you think?

I'm guessing that's what you want: 'peace of mind' 'financial security' and 'financial independence'.

Or, is there something more important?

In fact, is there some 'thing' that is so incredibly important that it actually DETERMINES 'peace of mind', 'financial security' and 'financial independence'?

It's something REALLY important.

Let me tell you what it is.

But first, to help me make my point, I'd like to prove something to you.

Becoming Financially Independent is easy.

I can show you how you could become totally financially independent pretty well immediately. In the process I can show you how you can also have total financial security AND total peace of mind.

Are you interested?

Are you up for it?

All you need to do is this …

FIVE STEPS TO FINANCIAL INDEPENDENCE

Step 1: sell your car, or sell your house, assuming you have one.

Step 2: with the proceeds, get yourself a cheap flight out to Kathmandu, Nepal.

Step 3: take a short cheap internal flight out of Kathmandu to Lukla. You'll enjoy the landing experience.

Step 4: pop on your walking boots and head North. You'll eventually come to a little village called Jorsalle, on the west side of the Dudh Kosi river, just south of Namche Bazaar, in the spectacular Khumbu region.

Step 5: Take a right turn. You'll now be off the beaten track. After another 30 minutes, you'll come to another little village. Your new home! Here you can buy yourself a little shack for next to nothing. What's more, with most of the sale value of your car or house still in the bank, you'll probably be the richest person in the village!

There you go. You're now sorted for the rest of your life!

You may have to walk half a mile or more for your water, but you WILL be financially independent for the rest of your life! You will also have total financial security - and you'll also be in the perfect place to find real peace of mind!

See how easy achieving financial independence can be?

Ah, you say … "What!!! I have to walk half a mile for my water!? I'm not sure about that! And what about my car? I quite like my car, thank you very much. I don't want to go without that! And what about my golf club? And my high tech music system? I can't listen to my favourite music on anything less than my top-of-the-range Bang & Olufsen!"

So, all of a sudden, what was just easily achievable, now becomes a lot more difficult. The 'price tag' of financial independence has just gone up - because of just one thing: LIFESTYLE.

FACT: When it comes to planning your financial future, THE most important factor is the cost of your current and future desired lifestyle. That's what makes - or breaks - any financial plan. Yet it is the one factor most often overlooked, even by financial professionals.

Quite simply, a big lifestyle can mean a big problem, a little lifestyle can mean a little problem: a big lifestyle requires a big Number; a little lifestyle a lesser Number.

Think about it. Lifestyle is everything. It's what you live for. It's what you bust a gut for - day in, day out - to create a better life for you and your family.

Lifestyle: it's the way you choose to live your life - OR the way you choose NOT to live!

It's identifiable. It's what you do. It's about what you want to do.

It's also about what you DON'T want to do, and what you will pay to avoid doing those things. After all, that's why you have a private jet, right?

It's the cost of your holidays in the Maldives. It's the cost of your housekeeper or nanny. It's the cost of your gardener. It's the cost of your tennis court and swimming pool and their ongoing maintenance, it's the cost of privately educating little Tommy and Theresa at St. Trinian's. It's the cost of your flying lessons and restoring your vintage Bentley.

I jest.

It could just be the cost of living a simple life, in Newcastle - or in Nepal.

The fact is, it's different for each of us. Only you know the cost of your lifestyle. And it's probably time you gave it some thought. So, in the next chapter I'll help you to do so.

Be warned though! I'm not talking here about creating a budget! No way!

Budgets aren't fun. A budget is where you spend the same money this month as you did last month. That's no way to live!

No. I'm talking about you designing, creating - and keeping - a life worth living!

I'm talking about you getting a handle on the cost of your lifestyle so you can plan to maintain it, or make it better. You decide.

If you haven't got a clue how much you spend, then it's time for me to give you a shake!

Financial independence is being in such a position that if you work beyond a certain date, it's because you want to, not because you have to. It's about having sufficient resources to maintain your future desired lifestyle without risk of ever running out of money.

It's about having ENOUGH!

KEEPING your desired lifestyle and NOT running out of money is the key!

You see, anyone can have a great lifestyle temporarily. All you need is half a dozen credit cards! Or better still, just keep remortgaging your house every few years. That is exactly what a large percentage of the population have been doing in recent years, helped, up until recently, by easy access to credit.

In fact, for many years it has been easier to take out a credit card and spend money that you haven't got than it is to put money aside for your future. To take out a savings plan for your future you need to prove your identity, and follow strict Money Laundering rules! Not exactly a great way to encourage saving for your future. But a credit card, or that new mobile phone contract, it just takes a few clicks of your mouse!

The trouble with the easy credit culture that so many people have got used to, is that it creates a situation where many people can't afford the lifestyle they have now - while they are still working - let alone when they stop work and the money stops coming in. Some people are just going to have to get used to living on less. A lot less!

Just make sure it's not you!

Don't think of me as shallow. I'm not suggesting for one minute that your lifestyle and how much you spend is the most important thing in life! No way. But when it comes to successfully planning your financial future it definitely is THE most important thing. Period.

I once heard it said that *"Money isn't the most important thing in the world, but it's high on the list, right up there with oxygen!"*

The fact is, with it you can do a lot. Without it, you're stuffed!

What's important is getting enough of it to satisfy your needs. And that's where the problem starts.

What are your REAL needs? What do you REALLY want?

Starting to think about your lifestyle, and the cost of maintaining it, can be an eye opener to something much deeper.

Remember, I'm not talking here about you having more, more, more. Not at all.

I'm talking about LIVING BIG and LIVING RICH.

Living BIG and living RICH can often be about you NOT having more, more, more. It can be about you having less, less, less! It can be about you quitting your £400,000 a year job in the City - a job that perhaps no longer fulfils you - to go and live on a smallholding in the country, earning very little - but being really happy and fulfilled doing what you love. That's living rich.

You live big by following your heart, by following your passion. Living rich can mean devoting your life to breeding a brand new type of rose or teaching yoga.

The question is, what do you want your financial future to look like? In particular your desired lifestyle. Only you can answer that.

"But I don't know what I want?"

One of the most common things new clients have said to me in my years as a Lifestyle Financial Planner is this:

"The trouble is Paul, I don't really know what I want - so how can I plan my future?"

My answer to that is simple. You might not know what you want, few people do - and that's OK. But I'll bet that you do know what you DON'T want! And what you don't want is probably *'nothing less than what you have right now'.* Am I right?

Therefore, the starting point in creating any financial plan is to identify what you have now, in other words your CURRENT LIFESTYLE. This becomes the starting point for planning the rest of your life and achieving financial independence. We can then plan to make adjustments to your lifestyle costs (perhaps in later life) through choice, rather than by being forced to make those changes.

The way we do this is by getting to grips with what your current lifestyle looks like and how much it costs you. We do this by going through a simple lifestyle expenditure questionnaire. This data can then help you to look at the cost of various stages of your life, to see how it might change. I will expand on this later.

Planning your financial future successfully is all about waking up right now to the cost of the life you have. It's about comparing that to the life you want and the life you don't want - and understanding the cost of each.

Chapter Fourteen

What If You Are There Already?

There's a little story I sometimes used to tell my clients, it's called *"The Mexican Boatman"*

It's a great little story. So much so, that when I first heard it, it changed my personal definition of 'success'.

The story goes as follows ...

There was a high powered Management Consultant, who had a Harvard MBA, on holiday on a beach in Mexico.

Early one morning he saw a local boatman come up to the shore in his little boat. Inside the boat was a large yellow fin tuna. He got talking to him and he said to the boatman: *"Tell me what you do with your life?"*

The Mexican said, *"Well, I go out fishing early in the morning and I catch a yellow fin tuna. I come back and I sell it, then I go home, have breakfast or an early lunch with my beautiful wife. We chat a while. Most days we make love followed by a snooze in the afternoon. Then in the early evening, I play with the kids when they get back from school, I have dinner with my wife and then I go down to the local cantina where I play guitar, sing and have a drink with my amigos!"*

The Management Consultant said: *"I think I can help you, because I have a Harvard MBA. Here's my advice: instead of coming back so early, why don't you stay out and fish a little longer and catch more tuna. That way you can make more money so you can buy a bigger boat."*

"Really?" said the Mexican. *"Then what happens?"*

"Well, then you can catch even more fish. Then what you can do is employ some of your amigos and set up a fishing fleet to catch even more yellow fin tuna!"

"Wow!" the Mexican said, *"... and then what happens?"*

"Well ..." said the Consultant, *"Eventually, you can bypass the middle man altogether and have your own cannery! Over the years you can build a fantastic fleet and a marvellous business!"*

The Mexican was fascinated by all this and he said, *"That is brilliant, what happens next?"*

"*Well, eventually, you'll have thousands of employees, you will have to move to a new Head Office in New York. Then what we'll do is we will help you do an IPO and sell the business and make millions!*"

...and the Mexican said, "*How many millions?*"

The Consultant said, "*Well ... about twenty!*"

So the Mexican says, "*Wow! Twenty million! What happens then?*"

And the Consultant says: "*Oh, that is the best bit! You can then relax, retire to a little Mexican fishing village and in the morning you can get up and go fishing for a yellow fin tuna and in the evening you can play guitar and have a few drinks with your amigos!*"

When I first heard that story, it stopped me in my tracks.

I thought really hard about it.

It was one of those great lessons in life. I suddenly realised that I already had some of the success I was looking for. I had reached where I wanted to be. I just wasn't capitalising and maximising or thinking about the wonderful life that I had already got. I got caught in the trap of wanting more, more, more.

The moral of the story is, you might already have the life you really want. So why work harder or longer than you really need to?

Something to think about, eh?

Remember, it's about LIVING BIG and LIVING RICH - and that has very little to do with money.

It's all about knowing 'How Much Is ENOUGH?'

Let's now find out what's going to happen to your bucket, and what you can do about it.

Chapter Fifteen

Relax. It's Easier Than You Think!

It's time to find out what's going to happen to YOUR bucket.

Would you like to see what your financial future might look like, so you can work out for yourself, how much is enough?

It really is easier than you think.

If you are competent with numbers and spreadsheets, you can produce a financial forecast using Microsoft Excel to identify what's going to happen to your bucket. You'll need to be careful with your formulas and your assumptions, but if you are up for the challenge and don't mind putting in a few hours of concentrated effort using Excel, then the following chapters will help you piece this spreadsheet together.

Or, you could take an easier option.

Luckily there is an alternative method of forecasting your financial future - a shortcut - that will make this exercise far simpler - and a lot more fun!

To help you crunch your numbers and find out what is going to happen to your bucket, you can use a new piece of simple, user friendly software called **'Envision Your Money'** (www.envisionyourmoney.com). Quite simply, it helps you to 'envision' what your financial future looks like.

It has been developed to save you hours of messing around with spreadsheets and worrying about whether you have used the right formulae etc.

Furthermore, **'Envision Your Money'** is based totally on the bucket concept.

Unlike a spreadsheet it will actually show you what will happen to your bucket as your circumstances change. It keeps things simple. It also includes video instruction to help you create your own financial plan. Furthermore, as a reader of *'Enough?'* you will receive a discount if you go to: www.envisionyourmoney.com/enoughbook.

If you are one of the lucky few who has experienced PROPER financial planning from a PROPER Financial Planner - who delivers advice using comprehensive financial forecasting software - then you'll already know the clarity it provides can be life changing. As discussed already, knowing what your bucket looks like can facilitate all sorts of life enriching decisions.

But it is not just a select few that deserve this clarity!

I believe that EVERYBODY needs to know what's going to happen to their bucket.

I'm also aware that not every person wants or can afford to employ the services of a professional financial planner. So that's why my team and I have created **'Envision Your Money'**. Now, there is no reason why you can't have a go at doing it yourself.

'Envision Your Money' is designed to take you through all the simple steps you need to get an overview of your financial future. There is even video instruction to explain each simple step, so I am quite literally able to talk you through the whole process. It's really easy to use. It will give you a real 'feel' for what's going to happen to your bucket. It will get you thinking about your financial planning in a new way and give you more clarity than ever before.

So, whether you have decided to try **'Envision Your Money'**, or to go ahead and do it yourself - congratulations! You are well on your way to getting a better understanding of your financial future.

On the other hand, you might have already decided that now you understand the bucket concept you would prefer help from a professional financial planner who is trained in this concept.

If so, please go to:
www.envisionyourmoney.com/findadviser

This will put you in touch with a trusted member of our panel in your area who will be able to assist you.

Chapter Sixteen

What's In? What's Out?

The starting point is knowing what's inside and what's outside your bucket. This will help you to identify your Net Worth.

Remember, money inside your bucket is money that is 'liquid'. It's easily realisable. It's accessible. It's money you can get hold of at any time, normally within 7-10 days. This means you can spend it. It's YOUR money.

Money outside your bucket is still your money, but you can't spend that money UNTIL you sell these assets. Sometimes you can't (or don't want to) sell these assets.

Money inside your bucket will include the following:

Cash
Bank Deposit Accounts
Building Society Accounts
Individual Savings Accounts (ISAs)
Cash value of Savings Plans
Cash value of Endowment Policies
Investment Portfolios
Stocks & Shares
Gilts
Investment Bonds
Etc

Money outside your bucket will include:

Value of your current home (after deducting any outstanding mortgage)
Value of any other property (after deducting any outstanding mortgage)
Private Pension Funds
Company Pension Funds in your name.
Business value - your share value of your business (but ONLY IF POSSIBLE TO BE SOLD - see Chapter Twenty - A Special Word to Small Business Owners).
Other assets that you intend to sell one day (e.g. yacht, antiques, stamp collection)

Depreciating assets such as cars etc. should be ignored, as should general house contents etc.

Debt

Let's keep this simple for now. For the sake of this initial 'net worth' exercise, just deduct the amount of outstanding debt from the value of the relevant assets (e.g. deduct any mortgage outstanding on your home from the realistic value of your home to give your net equity in your home).

For a simple Net Worth Summary for you to use, please go to www.envisionyourmoney.com/tools where you will find a Net Worth Summary for you to download and complete. It will add up all the figures for you.

Once completed, these figures can then be easily inserted directly into **'Envision Your Money'**. Simple to follow videos will show you how.

Assumptions

When it comes to planning your financial future, you will need to allow for growth on your invested assets, i.e. the expected investment return you are likely to achieve on your savings and investments. My advice is to be very conservative with your assumptions. It's easy to 'hope' that your investments will achieve 8-10% or more per year in investment return over the long term - but chances are they won't. Furthermore, the more risk you take with your investments the more likely you are to suffer a serious loss caused by a market fall or economic crisis at some point in the future.

My advice when initially planning your financial future is to err on the side of caution. Plan with prudence in mind, not performance. Apply this same caution when it comes to predicting increases in the value of your home, or any other asset. If you are a small business owner, be realistic about how much you hope your business will be worth in the future. Remember, if you can't sell it, you can't spend that money! (Please See Chapter Twenty - A Special Word To Small Business Owners.)

Relying on an expected inheritance

Relying on the future distribution of your parents' estate may not be a sensible financial plan. Who is to say you will ever get it? What if your parents live longer than you expect? What if your inheritance is eaten up by their medical expenses and/or long term nursing care? Not to mention Inheritance Tax / Estate Taxes. Planning to be financially dependent on an inheritance can be a foolish plan. Having said that, an 'allowance' can be made for sums that 'might' arise. But my suggestion would be to at least halve the expected amount - and plan on receiving it 10 to 20 years later than you first forecast.

Relying on a future house downscale

Many people believe that their financial future will be secured just by moving to a smaller house and living off the proceeds.

The relevant point here is do you want to be financially dependent on the future sale of your home? Do you want to end up selling your house because you have to, or because you want to? The same rules as above apply.

Factoring in an intended future house downscale to a financial plan can be a reasonable thing to do and can make a big difference to 'what's possible'. However, when it comes to planning your financial future, don't be over ambitious with expectations of future house price increases.

Be conservative - and then you won't be disappointed.

Once you've got a good idea about how much you are worth, and what is inside your bucket and how much is outside your bucket, we can then start considering what's coming into your bucket both now and in the future, which we'll do in the next chapter.

Great news! You have taken your first steps towards creating your own financial plan!

Chapter Seventeen

What's Coming In To Your Bucket?

We now need to identify what inflows are coming into your bucket now and how long these inflows will last. We also need to consider what FUTURE inflows will start, when and also how long those will last.

Your CURRENT inflows will include your NET (after tax) take home pay (salary, wages etc) for yourself and/ or your partner and any other incomes coming in now, (e.g. child benefit if applicable, or dividend income from a business (net of tax) or NET rent from any Buy To Let properties you may own, etc). You will need to consider at what age you expect these current inflows to stop and also if they are expected to increase each year or stay level.

The same applies to FUTURE inflows. These will include such things as: expected state pension for yourself and/or your partner; any personal pensions; any employer pensions. Again, these should be estimated for now (using conservative assumptions to be on the safe side). As you get more of an idea of what this all means you can then start to dig deeper into your figures and make them more accurate. This will provide you with more peace of mind and open up countless opportunities, perhaps to spend more, or save more.

You'll also need to think of any ONE OFF inflows that may be due to you. This is where you would input cash received from a planned house downscale, the sale of a second property, or from a possible inheritance, etc. Remember, exercise prudence in these predictions.

For a simple to use Income Summary which will help you to identify and total up your sources of income please go to www.envisionyourmoney.com/tools where you will find a simple 'Income Summary' for you to download and complete.

Once identified, these inflows can then be easily input into **'Envision Your Money'** (by following the simple videos) or included as inflows on your spreadsheet if you choose to use Excel etc.

You will need to exercise caution when using a spreadsheet. One thing you will need to consider is inflation. Are these inflows expected to increase every year? Will they increase at the same rate as inflation? (So they keep their buying power?) Will they increase at a rate higher than inflation? Or will they stay level? (i.e.

they are a fixed income - such as a fixed annuity). If any of your incomes stay level then they will lose purchasing power over the years ahead as the effects of inflation erode its value.

If you use 'Envision Your Money' it will automatically help you to allow for inflation. It will help you identify whether incomes increase or stay level, and you can apply an estimated rate of increase, either at your default rate of inflation or whatever rate of increase you feel is relevant.

BE CONSERVATIVE

The key is always be conservative in your assumptions! We would all like to think that our income will increase every year by 10 or 20%. But chances are it won't. Remember, when you start to get an idea of where you are heading using conservative assumptions, you can easily revisit your assumptions and create additional 'what if' scenarios which might allow for slightly more optimistic expectations regarding growth in income or investments.

Once you've got a good idea of what is expected to be coming into your bucket, at various stages of your life, then it's time to turn our attention to the fun part! How much do you expect to SPEND! In other words, how much will you be expecting to go out of your bucket, at various stages of your life, to give you the lifestyle you require or desire.

That's covered next.

Chapter Eighteen

What's Going Out Of Your Bucket?

Once you have a really good idea of what's currently in your bucket, what's outside of your bucket, and what will be coming into your bucket at various stages of your life things will be starting to make sense. (If you're using **'Envision Your Money'** you will now be able to see a graphical representation of this).

Now it's time to think about your current and future expenditure requirements. Again, this is easier than you might think.

Getting a fix on how much you spend can be truly enlightening. It can give you power! In fact, I'd like this to be a positive experience for you. Financial planning needn't be boring or scary! Once you know how much you spend you can take control. Not knowing how much you spend is what always causes problems.

Remember, we are not talking here about a 'budget' as such. We're talking about designing and achieving your desired lifestyle! This could be planning to spend MORE on things that matter - and less on things that don't. We're talking about YOU getting and keeping the life you want.

We are looking here at what you CURRENTLY spend to live a good life (hopefully). We then use this information to help us compare how much you are likely to need to spend in the future to maintain a good life (or have a better one).

An Expenditure Summary can be downloaded free of charge at www.envisionyourmoney.com/tools. If you use this it will add up all the columns for you and summarise the various categories of expenditure. You can then easily transfer the summarised figures into 'Envision Your Money' or your excel spreadsheet.

Here's a quick snapshot....

EXPENDITURE SUMMARY QUESTIONNAIRE

	TAP 1 Current Lifestyle	TAP 2 At Active Retirement	TAP 3 Later Retirement
Housekeeping Expenses	NOTE: Keep figures in today's pounds!		
Electricity			
Gas			
Water Rates			
Council Tax			
Home Telephone			
Repairs & Renewals			
Solid Fuel			
Oil			
Garden/Gardener/Plants etc			
Help in House			
House & Contents Insurance			
Other Insurance			
TV Licence			

So, in the Expenditure Summary you will see THREE columns.

The first column represents your CURRENT lifestyle, i.e. thinking back to your bucket, this is your FIRST TAP. How much do you currently spend per year in these areas to sustain your current lifestyle? It's time to have a go at getting a good grasp on this. Don't be scared.

The second column represents your DESIRED FUTURE lifestyle. This is your SECOND TAP which is the tap you will turn on when you retire, (or semi retire) etc. This is when you will have a lot more time to enjoy yourself, to travel more, take up hobbies, etc.

Here's the good news: if you fill in the first column first (current lifestyle) it will be much easier for you to complete this second column. All you need to do is compare how much you will expect (or require) to spend in your early retirement years compared to now. Bear in mind, these are the retirement years in which you will be likely to have the most fun - while you are still fit and able to do stuff! Remember, life's not a rehearsal!

So, some of your current expenses will go down when you turn on TAP 2, and some will go up. And that's OK!

IMPORTANT NOTE: If you are already retired, you should ignore the first column (FIRST TAP) and go straight to the second column. Remember, these should be ANNUAL figures.

TIP: If you need any help identifying these figures it is a good idea to look at previous bank statements and credit card statements. Don't forget to include things that you pay for with cash! Keep a look out for your regular (or irregular) cash withdrawals from the hole in the wall (ATM). Be realistic and be honest with yourself. You'll be glad you did.

The THIRD column represents your THIRD TAP. If you recollect, this is the stage in your life when your needs change. This is the stage of your life when you become *'too old to enjoy yourself'*. I don't intend for that to sound flippant. You simply won't be able to do the sort of things you used to do. The reason why I want you to allow for this fact is because if you can accept that you will be physically less able to do things later it often means you can do more stuff NOW! Use this column to adjust for less holidays, perhaps. Or a smaller car, or perhaps running a smaller home if you intend to downscale. Of course, you might want to make an allowance for other additional expenses though, like health care, prescriptions, eventual care home fees, etc.

Remember, the Expenditure Summary can be down-loaded free of charge at www.envisionyourmoney.com/tools. It will add up all the columns for you and summarise the various categories of expenditure. You can then easily transfer the summarised figures into **'Envision Your Money'** or your excel spreadsheet.

If you need some help filling this in, just watch the videos at **'envisionyourmoney.com'** which will talk you through it and help you work it all out.

ONE OFF EXPENSES

As we discussed earlier, there are likely to be large 'one off' expenses at certain stages of your life. Maybe, a son or daughter's wedding, perhaps a special holiday, or the purchase of a holiday home, yacht, etc.

Whatever the expense, it's likely to have a serious effect on what's going to happen to your bucket!

Again the Expenditure Summary (freely available at www.envisionyourmoney.com/tools) has a space for you to put a provision for these items, the amount you will require and an estimated date you'll need the money.

Remember, you can easily insert these figures into **'Envision Your Money'** (or your own spreadsheet) to see the effect on your bucket. The same applies to one off inflows - such as money realised from a house downscale or sale of business etc.

Chapter Nineteen

Not Enough? Are You Paying Yourself First?

*"People often say they can't afford to save.
The fact is, it's the 'other stuff' they can't afford"*

If you're still working; how much are you, personally, tucking away for your future?

Here's a fact. When it comes to money, there are two types of people.

Firstly, there are those who spend first and TRY to save what's left.

You've guessed it! There never is anything left. An unsatisfactory future is their only option. Period.

Then there are those who SAVE FIRST - and live on what's left. These are the ones who create financial independence for themselves and their families.

Here's the funny thing: the ones who save first and spend what's left, don't seem to go without. They somehow manage to live a great life on 'what's left'. Better still, they are free to spend 'what's left' - without feeling guilty!

So which camp do you fall into?

Don't put it off any longer!

Imagine you feel like you're nearly ready to retire, so you sit down to figure out if you have enough money to live comfortably. You're crunching away and ... whoops! You find out that you have enough money to live for just 4 years and 7 months! What are your options? Continue working? Die young? Get a part-time job at B&Q? Move in with the kids?

The point is this: We all have one shot at saving for our future. If we blow it, we don't get to go back and do it over again. Procrastination is the thief of time.

What are you doing right now to accumulate wealth for your future?

Remember, the best time to start proper saving was 20 years ago. The second best time is today.

Make 'paying YOURSELF first' a part of your life.

There's a wonderful little book I can thoroughly recommend. It contains the important wealth-building secrets that are brought to life in the classic, best-selling parable *"The Richest Man in Babylon,"* by George S. Clason.

Let's examine one of those secrets in detail.

The Richest Man in Babylon, Part 2: Pay Thyself Today and Rest Easy Tomorrow

In the second chapter of "The Richest Man in Babylon," we meet Arkad, *"far and wide famed for his great wealth. He was generous in his charities . . . with his family . . . in his own expenses . . . but nevertheless each year his wealth increased more rapidly than he spent it."*

Arkad had learned a lesson about wealth building from his mentor, Algamish. That is when his fortune changed.

Algamish had told him, *"I found the road to wealth when I decided that a part of all I earned was mine to keep. And so will you."*

"But all I earn is mine to keep, is it not?" Arkad demanded.

"Far from it," Algamish replied. *"Do you not pay the garment maker? Do you not pay the sandal maker? Do you not pay for the things you eat? Can you live in Babylon without spending? What have you to show for your earnings of the past month? What for the past year? Fool! You pay to everyone but yourself. Dullard, you labour for others. As well be a slave and work for what your*

master gives you to eat and wear. If you did keep for yourself one-tenth of all you earn, how much would you have in 10 years?"

"As much as I earn in one year," Arkad replied.

"You speak but half the truth," Algamish retorted. *"Every gold piece you save is a slave to work for you. Every copper it earns is its child that also can earn for you. If you would become wealthy, then what you save must earn, and its children must earn, that all may help to give to you the abundance you crave.*

"Wealth, like a tree, grows from a tiny seed. The first copper you save is the seed from which your tree of wealth shall grow. The sooner you plant that seed, the sooner shall the tree grow. And the more faithfully you nourish and water that tree with consistent savings, the sooner may you bask in contentment beneath its shade."

And that was the beginning of Arkad's journey to wealth.

It's called *"paying yourself first."* It's an idea that is at the base of many of the best modern wealth-building programs.

It's a very simple idea. The money you spend on the trappings of wealth - cars, boats, jewellery, etc. - may make you feel wealthy, but they don't add to your wealth; they subtract from it. If you want to increase your wealth, there is only one way to do that: You must save and if you want to save regularly and effectively you should put a portion of your income into savings first - BEFORE you spend it on anything else.

Making the conversion from a spender to a saver isn't easy. It takes more than simply reading this book and saying to yourself, *"Yes, that's true. I know that."* It takes commitment and the discipline to follow a carefully articulated savings-and-investment plan over time.

The first thing you need to do is decide how much of your income you will *"pay yourself first."* That number, as Clason suggests, should be at least one-tenth of your income and can be *"as much as you are comfortable with."*

And it has to be done consistently with each and every paycheque and every time you bring in any extra income.

This is a profoundly important point. You have to make *"paying yourself first"* a regular habit - because until it becomes a habit, it is a chore.

The purpose of wealth building is not the acquisition of wealth itself but the power and peace of mind it can bring you. Unless and until you make paying yourself first an automatic part of your day-to-day routine, you won't enjoy those benefits.

Pay yourself first. Invest 10% . . . 20% . . . 30% of your income, as you get it, and within a relatively short amount of time (two years, three years, or maybe five years, but certainly not longer), you'll experience a complete change in the way you think about money.

You'll no longer count your wealth by recounting your possessions. You'll see your material trappings as what they are - toys that give you temporary pleasure. And you'll begin to see your savings/investment nest egg for what it is - a true measure of your potential to live life to the fullest.

Just start. NOW!

Chapter Twenty

A Special Word to Small Business Owners...

If you run your own small business, either as the sole owner, or as a partner or co-director, you have an incredible opportunity that must be maximised.

You have an asset that could help you accumulate ENOUGH!

But first, let me ask you a question….

Have you ever bought a ticket from British Airways?

Have you ever looked really closely at it?

Next time you buy a ticket, I want you to look really closely at it. Really, really closely.

In particular, look in the bottom right hand corner.

If you look really closely, with your best reading glasses on - or preferably with a magnifying glass - you will see something hugely important....

Hidden, almost in the fibres of that paper ticket (even if you printed it online) you'll see, in the smallest print imaginable, built into the ticket, these words....

"Ticket price includes the cost of retirement of Pilot and Cabin Crew"

It's all built into the ticket!

What I'm getting at here is British Airways have incorporated into the price of their tickets the cost of providing for the retirement of their key staff.

The question for you, as a small business owner, is have you built in to the price of your 'tickets' the cost of your future? (i.e. your 'tickets' are your widgets, your products, or your service.)

British Airways have - so why not you?

In my 25 year's experience I've found that many business owners build into the price of their tickets / widgets / service the cost of their staff, their premises, their heating, lighting, stationery and toilet rolls, but most fail to build into their prices the cost of their own future!

What about YOU?

Your future is an overhead! Probably one of the most important overheads you've got. But it's easy to forget it and it MUST be built into the price of what you sell. No one else is going to do it for you.

So, the starting point for YOU (if you are a business owner) is to crunch some numbers. Work out how much is ENOUGH, and how much you need to accumulate each year. Start making that an important overhead in your business. You owe it to yourself.

Here are a few more mistakes business owners or anyone thinking of starting a business need to avoid.

Relying on a Business Sale

Many business owners factor into their financial future the possible sale of their business. The first question you need to ask yourself though is: *"Is my business a 'sellable business', or an 'owner dependent' business?"*

A 'sellable' business is a business that functions superbly without depending on the day to day, week to week, month to month input of the owner. The owners are mere shareholders in the 'corporate entity' that delivers the results of the business.

If you are a business owner there is an easy way to find out whether you have one of these businesses! Just ask yourself the question: *"If I take 6 to 12 months off to go sailing (or whatever) will my business still exist when I get back?"*

If your honest answer to this question is yes, (assuming you haven't been running the business remotely via satellite phone!) then chances are you have a very 'sellable' business - the business doesn't depend on you.

But if your answer is no, then think again.

If you do have a sellable business (or you can definitely make the changes necessary to turn your business into a sellable business) then an allowance for the realistic sale proceeds of your business can be made as a future inflow into your bucket. But my advice is to always err on the side of caution: it's your future we're talking about! Do not 'over value' your business or expect to receive that exact same sum on the exact same day that you need it. It rarely works out like that. Moreover, don't forget to allow for tax!

Always remember, that until such time as you physically sell your business, if you include it in your financial planning - if you believe that one day that money is going to come into your bucket - then you are planning to be financially DEPENDENT on that business.

Personally, I'd rather help people to plan to be financially independent - WITHOUT relying on the future sale of a business. That's because businesses and business sectors have a nasty habit of suffering from changing fortunes over time.

Look around your own local area at the successful businesses that once were! In the UK, what about those local, friendly DIY stores - completely wiped out by B&Q. Or those high street book and record shops whose death was Amazon and iTunes. Wherever you live in the world, it's easy to see examples of businesses that got wiped out.

Remember too, nothing undervalues a business (or any asset) more than the owners keenness to sell!

You see, if you can plan on being truly financially independent (i.e. without being reliant on the future sale of your business) you can then become detached from the outcome.

Something amazing then happens. This will result in a higher sale value: even though you don't really need it! More importantly, it will result in less stress for you and your family. Hey, that money from the sale of your business, it just becomes icing on the cake, you can buy a bigger boat!

The 'owner dependent' business, as you've probably guessed, is a business which continues to exist only because of the sheer constant physical, mental and emotional input of the owner. Michael Gerber in his book the E-Myth refers to these business owners not as entrepreneurs, but as technicians. They are technicians who once suffered from an entrepreneurial seizure which resulted in them starting their own business. It goes like this: One day they were working for somebody else, and the day comes when they think *"Why am I working for this idiot when I could work for myself and then make ALL the money?"*

So they quit their job and start their own business. They then find themselves working for an even bigger idiot:

themselves! Now they're doing all the technical work they used to do, plus all the other work, the accounts, marketing, HR, recruitment, managing the business etcetera etcetera. For many people the business takes over their life, they're busy just getting caught up in 'doing it, doing it, doing it' with the result that they have no life!

The chances of selling these type of business are slim. Why? Because any new owner needs to replace you (and the multiple roles you fill) and that will cost money. Alternatively, you might sell it, but the deal requires that you end up working for the new owner for three or more years. That's not so good! You'll possibly be no better off than if you kept it - and kept the future profits!

The point here is simple, for many people their business is their greatest asset, and so it should be. But it needs to work WITHOUT you, not because of you. It needs to work without you, the owner, doing the work. You need to work on it, not in it. Only then can you truly build it to sell it.

Again, when you understand your Number, i.e. how much is ENOUGH, you can start to engineer your business so it one day gives you freedom from the business. The book *'The E-Myth - Why small businesses don't work and what to do about it'* by Michael Gerber is a good starting point for great advice about building a business that you can sell.

So, when you are crafting your financial plan either using **'Envision Your Money'** or using your own spreadsheet, just be conservative about how much you expect your business to be worth in the future. Remember, if you sell it for more than you expect, it will be a bonus.

Chapter Twenty One

A Word About Investing

If you're planning your financial future there will obviously be times when you need to invest some money. If you already have a portfolio of investments, whether inside your bucket or inside your pension funds, you'll need to make sure these are working for you, not against you. They need to be supporting your bucket!

Here's where you can relax. This needn't be complicated. It should be as simple, painless, low cost - and as low risk - as possible.

However... the Financial Services Industry doesn't see it this way!

The Industry likes making things complicated. Very complicated. It just loves coming up with a constant flow of shiny new funds that they can sell to unwary investors. This drives their 'money-go-round'.

The Industry then spends billions each year promoting their sexy new funds - again aided by the financial porn that supports it.

What I'd like you to do is imagine a great big room ...

At one end of the room is you (and other people like you).

You'll all be wanting to receive an investment return of some kind on your money. Ideally, this return should be in line with the prudent requirements of your bucket.

Some people will require a low return (perhaps because they are a Got Too Much or a Just Right). Others might require a higher return.

At the other end of the room are the financial markets. These markets deliver an investment return over time. Some markets offer a low return, other markets offer a higher return. Risk and return are related. Never forget this. The more risk you're prepared to take the more return (and volatility) you can expect from the markets over time. The less risk you're prepared to take, then the less return (and volatility) you can expect over time.

Pretty good so far don't you think? We've got 'you' on this side of the room wanting a return, and over there we've got the 'investment markets' that deliver a return.

Sounds perfect.

The only trouble is, in the middle of the room - standing between you and the return you require - piled almost to the ceiling, is a great big pile of GOO. That GOO is the Investment Industry.

How good is your imagination? Because, if you listen very carefully to this great big pile of GOO, you'll hear a strange sucking noise.

That sucking noise is the sound of the Investment Industry sucking charges out of your money, with the result being that the return you require from the markets is rarely, if ever, achieved.

Why?

Because THEY rake out all their charges from your money!

Trading commissions, bid offer spreads, annual management charges, performance bonuses, platform costs, etc (the list goes on and on and on!) These charges fund this thing called 'the Industry' - including all the big posh offices, the big salaries, the gigantic bonuses; all the lawyers, the marketers, the billions in advertising costs, etc, etc, - it all comes out of your money.

The result being that you never quite get the return you deserve.

But guess what? Even if they do a bad job and your money goes down - they still take their charges!

Depending on the type of funds you hold you could be paying anything from 1.5% - 3% per annum to the GOO! In some cases, a whole lot more!

But there's a bigger problem. The GOO has recently got much, much thicker. Why? Because a whole new group of people have joined the GOO: Financial Advisers!

Many Financial Advisers, some desperately in need of a service proposition, are now parading as pseudo investment managers. In doing so they've added yet another layer of costs to the GOO. They can charge you an additional 1% a year for 'managing your money'! That's a lot of GOO!

The end result is that it's highly unlikely that you'll ever receive the return you truly deserve from the markets. There are too many layers of GOO! But it needn't be this way. There are ways of cutting out the GOO pretty much altogether. This can have a dramatic effect on your bucket and how much you need for the rest of your life.

The purpose of this brief chapter is NOT to educate you about the various investment possibilities or types of investments. That's not the purpose of this book! It is to draw your attention to the 'Industry Illusion' and to remind you that your money, in your bucket, is precious. So make sure you don't lose too much of it in high charges and unnecessary investment costs.

Investing your money for your future should be as simple, painless, low cost - and low risk - as possible. Don't let the Industry, or any Adviser, tell you otherwise.

Chapter Twenty Two

Risk and Investments

FACT: Millions of investors take far more risk than they need to take.

That is why, in recent years, millions of people have collectively lost billions of pounds in poor performing and risky investments. For a number of reasons, they had their money in all the wrong places. And it's still going on.

In the UK, the Financial Conduct Authority, the body set up to protect investors, is unwittingly leading financial advisers, investment providers and their clients astray!

THE PROBLEM

The root cause of this problem is that the Financial Services Industry relies far too much on 'risk profiling' as a method of recommending an investment solution to clients.

It goes like this …

Before selling you a financial product or investment, Advisers are supposed to ask you a series of questions to identify your 'risk profile' or your 'attitude to risk'.

This is rather like sticking pins in you to find out how much pain you can take. In other words they identify your 'pain threshold'.

They then recommend a product or investment to match your risk profile. In other words, they sell you a product or investment **designed** to give you that amount of pain - to keep you at or close to your pain threshold.

That's why many people could now be suffering that pain as they find themselves sitting on severe losses, because they may have been advised to take risks they didn't need to take.

Has this happened to you?

It's not a good way to get financial peace of mind, is it? Particularly in today's volatile investment markets.

It's completely wrong.

The Crucial Step That Most Investors
(and Advisers) Fail To Take

The starting point in any investment decision must always be where are you now and where are you trying to get to? This is the crucial step that gives meaning to any investment decision. But, sadly, it's the step that most investors - and those providing investment advice - fail to take.

In order to get to the right position an investor must first fully understand what they are trying to achieve. In other words, identify just how important their need for investment return is in the first place! Then, if it is important, the big question is what rate of return do you need? This can then determine the amount of risk, if any, you need to take.

The only real way to achieve this is through crunching the numbers to identify what's going to happen to your bucket, using conservative, prudent assumptions.

In other words, begin with the end in mind.

For example, perhaps like many people, your goal is to ensure that you can live the life you want without ever running out of money: a worthy objective!

So, what if you found out through Lifestyle Financial Planning that this could be achieved with a real rate of return on your invested capital of just 2% per annum? Why would you then risk your future by chasing higher returns? Why not just create a low cost, low risk, widespread, tax efficient portfolio designed to give you what you want: financial security and peace of mind?

What if, after allowing for all of your financial needs and all your expenditure requirements projected into the future, you discovered that you were never, ever going to run out of money? What if you found you could achieve ALL of your financial objectives WITHOUT taking any risk with your investments whatsoever? If that was the case, why on earth would you want to take any risk in the first place?

Conversely, if you found out that to achieve your objectives you needed a higher return - which required more risk - then you can decide to either take that risk, or possibly revise your objectives: for example, spend less in retirement, etc.

Remember, those in the Investment Industry want you to take risk. Otherwise, how are they going to get their hands on your money?

When you know what your financial future looks like you start to understand what level of return you really need to achieve. Then, and only then should you appraise your position relating to risk. Most people, and most Advisers, get this the WRONG way round.

It's 'not knowing' that causes people to invest with no rhyme or reason. The result being they invest in things they don't actually need that then do things they didn't expect. It's a major cause of financial stress in retirement and it costs investors dearly.

The Man Who Liked Financial Porn

I used to have a client who would constantly give me hassle. We had crunched his numbers and on really conservative assumptions he had more than enough money for the rest of his life. He was definitely a 'Got Too Much' - his bucket was NEVER going to run out!

So, we advised him to invest his money into a very cautious portfolio with very low risk. The mutually agreed long term objective of his financial plan was to ensure that he and his wife could continue to live a good life without worrying about ever running out of money.

When it came to investments, he was a perfect example of someone who didn't need 'performance'. He needed prudence and the peace of mind that comes with it. He needed a low but consistent return on his money with maximum peace of mind. The daily fluctuations and volatility of the stock market shouldn't really have ever concerned him.

But, after a few years, he found all this just a little boring. He kept seeing articles in newspapers, often written by unqualified financial journalists punting some advertiser's new fund. He kept hearing about his pals at the golf Club who were always keen to tell him about their recent investment successes and their recent big wins. (They never told him about their losses!)

So he told me that he had decided he wanted a better return. He wanted to take more risk. I disagreed.

Against my advice, he removed a large chunk of his portfolio and invested it with the schmoosing 'Wealth Manager' from the Private Banking division of his bank.

These 'Wealth Managers' were only too keen to give him some excitement - obviously in return for the extravagant 'management fees' they would be raking off his money.

To this day I don't know why I didn't sack him as a client there and then. But I continued to look after the rest of his money, sticking to the original plan.

What happened to his money with the 'Wealth Manager'?

At first he did OK. But then the markets dived, as they always do, sooner or later. He became increasingly stressed. He'd go on holiday with his wife, but she'd tell me that he'd be constantly distracted. His mind was always somewhere else. His body may have been on that deckchair, but his head certainly wasn't!

You see, instead of enjoying these precious moments with his wife on the beach, his head was stuck in the financial press worrying about the stock market! That's no way to have fun.

He then did what many people do. He panicked. He instructed his Wealth Manager to sell everything and go fully into cash until things settled down. (i.e. sell low). Six months later, when the markets had gone back up, he instructed them to reinvest (i.e. buy high).

That, my friend, is not how you 'manage wealth'. That is how you devastate wealth!

It's a sad fact, but millions of people stress over their money when they needn't. This is stimulated by the 'financial porn' (the consumer financial press) who want you to be frustrated with your money.

Financial journalists want you to be looking for the 'next new thing'. They want you to be unhappy with your returns. They want you to be searching for a better investment. Why? So they can keep advertising more of that stuff at you! All the while raking in millions in advertising revenue.

So, here's the key. Once you know your Number; once you know how much is ENOUGH, once you realise what's going to happen to your bucket, you can make smarter investment decisions. You can de-risk, and avoid paying excessive - and mostly unnecessary - investment costs. All of which is a no brainer.

Chapter Twenty Three

The Truth About Financial Advice

There is so much confusion surrounding financial advice. This is not helped by inherent conflicts of interest of some Advisers, not to mention the vested interests of the Financial Services Industry and the 'financial porn' that co-exists to support it.

Once you have a better understanding of your Bucket, about where you are heading financially, if you then decide you need an Adviser to help you, you will need to find an Adviser that suits your unique requirements.

Having a better knowledge of the distinction between Financial Planners and Financial Advisers will help you to make that choice.

Independent Financial Advice

It is supposedly the case that 'Independent' Financial Advisers or Planners are the only ones who are able to tailor solutions to a client's individual financial needs and objectives, based on an all-encompassing approach, impartial research and an ongoing working relationship.

Unfortunately, many 'independent advisers' or 'planners' - along with their 'restricted', 'tied' or 'multi-tied' counterparts, as they are known - are often little more than product salespeople. For some, their 'independence' simply means they are able to sell financial products from a larger range of providers.

Globally, the majority of 'Financial Advisers' are still paid by commission generated by selling financial products - or, more recently, by charging a percentage (e.g. 1% per annum) of all the clients' assets that they look after or 'manage'.

In the Industry, this system is called charging 'fees' on 'assets under management' or AUM. Many Advisers pride themselves on the size of their AUM - how much money they look after on behalf of their clients. It can be very lucrative. If they look after £100 million of their clients' money that's a million pounds in fees every year. (That's on top of the 1-3% they might charge every time they make an investment (or even switch investments) on behalf of their client).

Effectively, Advisers charging 1%pa have recently become the most expensive link in the investment distribution chain. They've become part of the GOO! Adding yet another layer of expense to be extracted from just one thing: your money.

But the big question is: what are they doing in return for their 'fees'? How are they making their clients' lives better?

It gets worse.

When people see an 'adviser' who plies their trade in a bank, building society, investment institution, or all too often, a large advisory practice, they are almost always seeing someone who is both unable to provide truly independent advice and who is probably paid by commission or bonuses of some description.

These environments are highly competitive and their bosses and/or shareholders need to be kept satisfied. As a result, there is a constant pressure to achieve sales and profitability targets. Ultimately, in these institutions, the quality of an 'adviser' is often measured by the number of sales they make, which of course presents potential conflict of interests. Those responsible for selling products to people know that unless they reach their targets, they will either not earn their bonuses, keep their jobs, or even be able to pay their mortgage.

The frustrating and confusing thing about this model is that it's often called 'advice'. Yet product sales have nothing to do with proper financial 'ADVICE'.

Financial Planners - v - Financial Advisers

The clue to the work professional Financial Advisers and Planners should do for their clients' is in their job titles: 'ADVISER' / 'PLANNER'. They should offer advice, construct and implement plans based on their client's real needs and objectives and the Adviser's advanced technical knowledge.

A Financial Adviser tends to provide 'product focused' advice: i.e. which pension, which investment, which ISA, etc.

A proper Financial Planner should provide 'planning' thereby giving more comprehensive advice taking into account ALL of your circumstances - lifestyle and long term objectives, assets, inflows, outflows - similar to how I described earlier. In other words, their job should be to show you what is going to happen to your bucket.

However this is rare. Unfortunately, many Advisers seem to call themselves 'Financial Planners' for one simple reason: because they are too embarrassed to call themselves a Financial Adviser!

Consequently, the problem is that many of the Advisers who call themselves Financial Planners DON'T do Financial Planning. It's not necessarily their fault. It's mainly due to the Industry's influence. They mostly transact products and investments - because this is what they've always done. It's how they get paid.

That's why, if you understand the concept of the 'Bucket', you probably already understand more about proper Financial Planning than many so called Financial Planners - and this puts you at a distinct advantage!

By the way, calling themselves a 'Wealth Manager' is also a good way to avoid the embarrassment of calling themselves a Financial Adviser!

So you have to be careful. It's not important what these financial types call themselves, it's what they can actually DO for you - their client.

In the context of looking after 'your bucket', financial products are often completely irrelevant to the financial planning process and are often not required. But of course, for someone who is paid by commission for selling or distributing financial products to people, there is a total emphasis on sales, and accumulating AUM. If they don't sell something they don't reach their targets, they don't earn money and they may lose their job.

It therefore isn't difficult to surmise that there is something potentially corrupting about the commission system - and the AUM system - which, globally, the majority of financial advisers work within.

It wouldn't be fair to say that there are no good commission or AUM percentage fee based advisers or planners out there. Of course there are! But it is also sadly true that there are still too many who give the good ones a bad name.

The best way to root out the lower quality Financial Advisers and Planners, and to drive up standards across the profession, is for consumers to insist on receiving

PROPER financial planning advice. Choose to work with those who deliver proper financial planning, ideally either Certified or Chartered Financial Planners - who are truly independent, who charge fees for their work and who work exclusively on behalf of their clients - and who deliver client focused 'Lifestyle Financial Planning' advice as outlined in this book. Any fees payable for comprehensive financial planning advice will be minuscule compared to the benefits received.

So how can I benefit from choosing an independent Financial Planner who delivers proper financial planning?

Proper Financial Planners get paid for their preparation of meaningful financial plans, for providing impartial advice, for their time and for the service they provide, just like a Solicitor or Accountant. They take care of your money, but they don't focus their work around selling you financial products. They work on your behalf NOT on behalf of the Industry. In fact, they should regard financial products (pensions, investments, ISAs, etc) as simply 'tools in their bag'. Nothing to get excited about. Just something to be used - IF and when necessary - to get the job done.

Any Adviser or Planner who is serious about working at the top of the profession and providing a high quality service to their clients will be truly independent, highly qualified and fee-based. That's a given.

Furthermore, if they are delivering proper Financial Planning, they will focus more on YOU than on your money.

Key points.

The financial planning process is about making long-term strategic decisions. So remember; you need a trusted Financial Planner - not a product salesman.

Don't use a Planner who can't explain things easily to you. You cannot simply delegate your financial planning, you must understand what your Planner is doing on your behalf. If they use jargon that you do not understand or make it all sound complicated then find a different Planner! Find someone who can explain it to you, so that you are part of the process. This is one of your best protections against poor advice.

Don't use a firm just because they are local. Because of technology, after the initial relationship is established, most people only need one detailed face to face meeting a year. If it means taking a day off and travelling once a year to meet with the right professional for you, then invest the time in doing this.

Remember, when you meet with a Financial Adviser or Planner, if they appear more interested in your money than they are in you, then it's time to run a mile.

Chapter Twenty Four

Finding The Right Adviser

If you feel you need the help of an Adviser, you should now understand the clear benefit of working with a suitably qualified 'Lifestyle Financial Planner' whose main focus is understanding you and what you are trying to achieve and then helping you to identify, achieve and maintain your desired lifestyle following the principles outlined in this book. They should also charge transparent fees for their service.

The fee based system helps to ensure that your chosen professional will not focus on the sale of financial products. Instead, they will focus on providing meaningful financial planning advice that revolves around you and what you are trying to achieve.

As you know already, the 'Lifestyle Financial Planning' process is designed to help you see what your financial future looks like. This service will simplify your financial life by helping you make sense of your money.

Hopefully, reading this book has already helped to illustrate that when you know where you're heading you can make smarter decisions about money.

Only then, when you and your Adviser truly know what is necessary, should any financial products or investments be transacted: i.e. for the RIGHT reasons. These products should simply be the 'tools' to enable you to achieve the objectives of your financial plan, ideally at the lowest level of cost and - more importantly - the lowest level of risk.

Remember, until an Adviser fully understands you and what you are trying to achieve - and only when they have helped you understand where you are heading financially - until then, they have NO right to sell you any financial product or tell you what to do with your money. Period.

Choosing the right adviser for you can be pretty daunting, especially when recommendations from well meaning friends can lead you into the same trap as our 'financial porn' loving friend from the earlier chapter.

The OTHER way?

I mentioned earlier that I had dedicated a good portion of my career developing a training course to share the methods and ideals of my business model. As a result of this there is now a growing community of highly qualified advisers who have embraced the best principles of good Lifestyle Financial Planning as outlined in this book. Most of them are qualified at the highest level in financial services, either Certified Financial Planners, Chartered Financial Planners, or both.

Some concentrate on specific vocations. There are Financial Planners who deal only with dentists, or lawyers for example, and therefore understand in great depth the specific demands on their industry or profession.

Most proper Financial Planning practices however, help clients from all backgrounds. There is now a good coverage of professional Lifestyle Financial Planners across Great Britain, Europe and worldwide.

If you want to connect with one of these advisers, who excel at delivering long term financial security and total financial peace of mind you can find out more by going here: www.envisionyourmoney.com/findadviser

They'll help you understand your bucket! They'll help you improve the efficiency of what's inside and what's outside your bucket. Where possible, they'll be able to help you make your money work harder now and in the future. They'll analyse your various inflows into your bucket and the tax efficiency of each and how this could be made better. And, of course, they'll help you analyse your expenditure requirements throughout life - to help you get peace of mind and create a 'life well lived'.

Remember: Life's not a rehearsal - so your financial prosperity should not be left to chance.

Case Study Six

This Case Study Is Quite Upsetting

I think the following story is really sad. It's a cautionary tale about what constitutes 'good advice'. It might explain my ongoing, often outspoken, frustration with the Financial Services 'Industry'. In particular, it might explain my criticism of Financial Advisers who miss the point when they fail to answer their clients' BIGGEST questions.

I hate going to funerals. I'll never forget that sad moment when I held the hand of Margaret, a newly widowed client. With tears in our eyes, we looked down into her husband's grave. It still grieves me to this day. There will always be a part of me that wonders if life could have been altogether different for them both.

John, her husband, had already been diagnosed with a terminal illness when they were referred to me by one of their closest friends, who was a client of mine. It was clear that John's main priority was to know that Margaret was going to be financially secure after he died.

In our first meeting, I soon discovered how, in my view, John and Margaret had been badly let down by their previous Adviser - a highly qualified 'Financial Planner'. This 'Financial Planner' wasn't really a 'Financial Planner' and had completely failed to identify their REAL needs.

At our meeting they passed me a report containing his recommendations from several years earlier. As I glanced through the report I could see that this 'Financial Planner' had obviously spent hours researching funds; he'd made recommendations that matched their risk profile perfectly, he'd produced a beautiful report to document his recommendation - and he'd then gone ahead and invested John and Margaret's money into Individual Savings Accounts (ISAs). He had done all of this professionally and in a timely fashion. I'd noticed he'd earned about four hundred pounds in fees/commission.

"So, where's the problem?"

Here's what he DIDN'T do...

All the 'Financial Planner' had done was satisfy John and Margaret's immediate need - for an ISA. But he HADN'T done any financial planning.

Sadly, because the Adviser had asked all the WRONG questions, he did not get to know what John and Margaret REALLY wanted. He arranged their ISA, but he failed to identify something really important: that both John and Margaret were, at that point, both working in a job they hated.

He'd only focused on the money that was available to invest, not on John and Margaret!

So, he hadn't asked the right questions. He hadn't bothered to find out about their goals and objectives; about their doubts and fears, worries and concerns.

He didn't find out what John and Margaret wanted out of life. He didn't identify the cost of their current and DESIRED lifestyle, he didn't crunch any numbers, and he didn't create a meaningful financial plan.

In short, he hadn't shown John and Margaret what was going to happen to their bucket!

So he failed to identify that, at that time, John & Margaret could have retired immediately and lived life to the full - without ever running out of money. They could have both left the jobs they hated and instead started having fun!

John and Margaret were *'Just Right'* types of clients. They already had enough money for the rest of their life - **but the problem was - like so many people - they didn't know that!!!!**

Worse though, the 'Financial Planner' hadn't bothered to find out. Quite simply, he'd failed to tell his clients the Truth About Money.

Sadly, three years later, John - still stressed and working full time in a job he hated - found out he'd got a brain tumour ... and just 6 months to live.

Tragically, if John had met with a 'Lifestyle Financial Planner', rather than just settle for traditional product focused 'advice', he may have decided upon early retirement ... he could have avoided the stresses and strains that came with his job - and this story may have had a much happier ending.

At the time, both John and Margaret regarded the service they received from the 'Financial Planner' as completely acceptable, in fact, they were happy with the advice they received. After all, they knew no different. Their 'Financial Planner' had broken no rules, he had facilitated the purchase of a product that he had assumed his client very much wanted. Unfortunately, he failed to realise the importance of helping his clients to understand their bucket. Had he done so, John's life might have changed fundamentally.

I believe the 'Financial Planner' concerned seriously failed his client. What do you think?

Personally, I believe it is every Financial Adviser's job to tell clients what I call 'The Truth About Money': to help them understand what's going to happen to their bucket.

Until that's done, whether they call themselves a Financial Planner, Financial Adviser or Wealth Manager, in my view, they have no right to sell you any form of financial product or tell you what to do with your money.

So, if you are in need of a financial advice, make sure the Professional you choose focuses on you and on what you want. Make sure they help you understand what's going to happen to your bucket BEFORE they talk to you about moving your money around or selling you new products or investments.

If you need help finding a suitable adviser who can deliver proper financial planning following the principles in this book, please go to *envisionyourmoney.com/findadviser*

Chapter Twenty Five

What's Most Important To You?

Thinking about your life and your money can uncover some deeper issues.

The following questions can get you thinking about what's really most important. If you're in a relationship it's a good idea to think about and answer these questions separately, and then discuss the answers together.

To help clients discover the deeper values in their lives, George Kinder, founder of the Kinder Institute of Life Planning poses three questions:

1. Imagine you are financially secure, that you have enough money to take care of your needs, now and in the future. How would you live your life? Would you change anything? Let yourself go. Don't hold back on your dreams. Describe a life that is complete and richly yours.

2. Now imagine that you visit your doctor, who tells you that you have only 5-10 years to live. You won't ever feel sick, but you will have no notice of the moment of your death. What will you do in the time you have remaining? Will you change your life and how will you do it? (Note that this question does not assume unlimited funds.)

3. Finally, imagine that your doctor shocks you with the news that you only have 24 hours to live. Notice what feelings arise as you confront your very real mortality. Ask yourself: What did you miss? Who did you not get to be? What did you not get to do?

Kinder says that answering the first question is easy. There are lots of things we'd do if money were no object. But as the questions progress, there's a sort of funnel. They become more difficult to answer, and there are fewer possible responses. Your highest truth comes from answering the third question.

Now some people ask, *"What does this have to do with money?"*

It has everything to do with money. When you understand what you want to do with your life, you can make financial choices that reflect your values.

So many of us are trapped in a world we hadn't quite planned for. But we can change it. These three questions can help you get to the bottom of what you really want, and so start on the path of designing the life you really want.

Remember, there'll come a time in everybody's life when they need to ask themselves three questions:

"Did I live?"

"Did I love?"

"Did I matter?"

I think the following piece sums it all up quite nicely. It was written by an eighty-five-year old who learned that they had just a few days to live...

"If I had my life to live over again, I'd try to make more mistakes next time. I wouldn't be so perfect. I would relax more.

*I'd limber up. I'd be sillier than I've been on this trip.
In fact, I know very few things that I would take seriously.
I'd be crazier. I'd be less hygienic.*

*I'd take more chances, I'd take more trips,
I'd climb more mountains,
I'd swim more rivers, I'd go more places I've never been to.
I'd eat more ice cream and fewer beans.*

I'd have more actual troubles and fewer imaginary ones!

You see, I was one of those people who lived prophylactically and sensibly hour after hour, day after day, year after year.

*Oh, I've had my moments, and if I had it to do over again,
I'd have more of those moments – moment by moment by moment.*

*I've been one of those people who never went anywhere without a
thermometer, a hot water bottle, a raincoat
and a parachute.*

If I had it to do all over again, I'd travel lighter next time.

*If I had it to do all over again, I'd start out earlier in the spring
and stay away later in the fall. I'd ride more merry-go-rounds,
I'd watch more sunrises, I'd play with more children…*

If I had my life to live all over again…

But you see, I don't!"

Isn't this a beautiful reminder? We only have so long on
this beautiful planet.

We have to make the most of it.

IN A NUTSHELL

Whatever your circumstances, no matter how much or
how little money you've got, understanding your money
and what's going to happen to your bucket, enables you
to take control and live life more fully.

Wow What A Ride!

Knowing what's going to happen to your bucket - how much is ENOUGH - is the best way to achieve financial security and financial peace of mind. It's also the best way of ensuring that you live the life you want.

I often remind myself of a quote by Hunter S. Thompson who said:

"Life should NOT be a journey to the grave with the intention of arriving safely in a pretty and well preserved body, but rather to skid in broadside, in a cloud of smoke, thoroughly used up, totally worn out, and loudly proclaiming "Wow! What a Ride!"

Remember how I mentioned earlier about lying on your deathbed with a mischievous grin on your face, while you giggle to yourself: *"That was so much fun!"*

Now is the time to start making this a real possibility!

We only get one life. Let's live it!

Chapter Twenty Six

Going To The Gym!

Now that you are close to finishing this book I really hope that you have taken these key elements away with you:

- You need to know how much is ENOUGH! For you.

- It's crazy to live this precious life worrying about money. Don't.

- Financial planning is all about 'knowing your bucket' and what's going to happen to it based on prudent assumptions.

- It's easier than you think to achieve financial independence. You might be there already. You need to know.

- If you're not there already, simple changes can make a big difference.

- The driver behind your bucket is your lifestyle.

- Big lifestyle = big number required. Little lifestyle = little number required.

- An 'awareness' of your bucket in your day to day helps you make smarter decisions about spending.

- Life's not a rehearsal. Enjoy life while you can.

- Life's too short to spend it doing something that does not make you happy. Change it.

- The starting point to living an extraordinary life is to refuse to live an ordinary one.

- It's no crime to be a 'Not Enough'. It is a crime to ignore it.

- Getting a feel for what's going to happen to your bucket is easy - **Envision Your Money** will show you how.

- There are simple steps you can take to calculate your inflows and outflows. I have included some worksheets and templates to download free of charge available to you at www.envisionyourmoney.com/tools.

I hope that this book will motivate you to want to take the first steps to securing your future. Whether you decide to work on it yourself, with the help of **'Envision Your Money'**, or via a professional you know you can trust, I genuinely believe that your life will be improved by utilising my bucket concept and taking these simple steps.

But here's something you MUST remember...

It's a fact: you can't go to the gym once and then be fit for the rest of your life! You have to keep going! Well, it's the same with Financial Planning! It's an ongoing process. You have to do it on an ongoing basis, year after year after year.

So, understanding your bucket and getting some clarity over where you are heading can give you a fantastic advantage, BUT you have to keep it under review. A 'One Off financial plan' won't work. Period.

Here's the thing: a client of mine, the airline pilot I mentioned earlier, confirmed to me that a 'plane taking off from London Heathrow bound for New York is actually off course around 95% of the time. Countless factors combine to constantly knock the airplane off course. The only reason it ends up in New York and not Zimbabwe is the auto pilot! The onboard navigation systems constantly correct course, pulling the 'plane back on track - so it finally gets to its destination.

It's the same with financial planning. It's an ongoing process. Things change - a lot. So you have to keep on top of it. Like the airplane, you have to constantly correct course - and that's easy when you have GPS. So think of **'Envision Your Money'** as your 'FPS' - your Financial Positioning System. Over time, little tweaks here. Little tweaks there. Then, the closer you get to your target, the easier it will be to hit.

The 'bucket' can be fun. With just a little awareness in your day to day thinking about your choices and actions - and their effect on your bucket - this can help you to stop wasting money so you build up your bucket. Of course, if you're a 'Just Right' or a 'Got Too Much' it will help you to see golden opportunities to enjoy your money and have some fun. Life's not a rehearsal.

I hope this book has helped you to think differently about your money and your future. I hope also that you've given **'Envision Your Money'** a try - to help you crunch YOUR numbers and see what your financial future might look like.

I've hopefully shown that financial planning needn't be boring. It can be inspiring and should be fun.

If you want to hear more from me, signing up to **www.envisionyourmoney.com/enoughbook** will put you on my mailing list. I will be sharing tips and ideas - and more case studies - to provide further inspiration. It will help keep you on your toes and make sure you're having fun - enjoying your money!

Remember, one life. Live it!

About the Author

Paul Armson has been a Financial Adviser since 1982. He started delivering 'Lifestyle' Financial Planning to *WOW* his clients in 1990 and built a small fee-based Financial Planning practice, primarily focusing on small business owners and retirees.

After the sudden death of his Mum he vowed to make *'Life's Not A Rehearsal'* his mantra and live life accordingly. He semi-retired at the age of 45 to start sailing his yacht *'Spellbound'* around the world with his soulmate, Lynn.

For the last eight years, when he's not been sailing, he's been helping other Financial Advisers successfully transition to a Lifestyle Financial Planning model.

Paul launched 'Inspiring Advisers' in 2013 - an online training programme to help more Advisers successfully adopt a Lifestyle Financial Planning approach. It is now a fast growing community of Lifestyle Financial Planners from the UK and around the globe.

Frustrated with the vested interests of the Financial Services Industry he now believes it's time to start telling consumers what he calls 'The Truth About Money'.

Paul is a sought after speaker and speaks regularly in the UK and overseas, he is passionate about changing clients and Advisers lives through the successful delivery of PROPER Financial Planning. Follow him on twitter @EnvisionYoMo.

Lightning Source UK Ltd.
Milton Keynes UK
UKOW02f1628160816

280803UK00001B/114/P